Praise for *The monkey-pro*

This book is genius, with Jonathan Lear – the man who brought us monkey sex and sought the promotion of Bob the brown trout to secretary of state for education – at his most irreverent and profound best.

Building from the basics, *The Monkey-Proof Box* both educates and entertains as Jonathan encapsulates the key ideas and processes that helped transform the challenging primary school where he works, and talks you through the design and delivery of a curriculum that systematically builds pupils' knowledge, creativity and independence.

Stephen Tierney, CEO, Blessed Edward Bamber Catholic Multi Academy Trust,
blogger and author of *Liminal Leadership*

The Monkey-Proof Box is an important book that unpicks many of the misconceptions about curriculum design and warns of the dangers of the 'ticking and clicking off' culture. It goes back to the essentials of the richness we want to be made available to all our pupils, and sets out how these can be accessed and assessed effectively – drawing on plenty of evidence from cognitive science to draw the threads together.

Crisp, cool and cutting on core curriculum principles, it's also very funny – and serves as a reminder to us all that we are more likely to bring people with us on our journey if we can laugh at ourselves.

Mary Myatt, education adviser, writer and author of *Curriculum: Gallimaufry to Coherence*

Any primary school teacher or head teacher weighed down by the unrelenting prescription of government but still seeking to excite the imaginations of their pupils will find Jonathan's book a stimulus in their search for what works in the classroom. A treasure trove full to the brim with creative and practical ideas around pedagogy and the primary curriculum.

Sir Tim Brighouse, former London Schools Commissioner and
Chief Education Officer for Birmingham and Oxfordshire

The Monkey-Proof Box takes the reader on a journey that, for an educational text, is unusually gripping and extremely readable. The book offers many useful insights that are in line with much of the current commentary on the importance of knowledge and the risks of teaching generic skills without also focusing on deep understanding. However, Jonathan makes this so much more accessible and meaningful in the way that he relates it to his own experience and therefore to practical application.

Professor Samantha Twiselton, Director, Sheffield Institute of Education, and
Vice President, Chartered College of Teaching

Having had the pleasure of working alongside Jonathan and listening to him speak at events, I am a huge advocate of 'going guerrilla' – and reading *The Monkey-Proof Box* has reminded me of exactly why I became a teacher.

Humorous and very relatable, this book is like every other encounter I have had with Jonathan: nothing short of brilliant!

Charlotte Smith, Teacher, Hartsholme Academy

The Monkey-Proof Box is a wonderful book that models innovation and social justice in education. Jonathan provides insights and anecdotes, models of alternative practice, and ideas and resources that fuse together principles and practice in a way that combines credibility and aspiration.

By turn wise and witty, reassuring and challenging, theoretical and practical, *The Monkey-Proof Box* provides a synthesis of what is possible in integrating our approach to teaching, learning and the curriculum.

A powerful resource for teachers and school leaders.

John West-Burnham, Visiting Professor, University of Suffolk

If you think you've thought about your curriculum, think and think again!

This inspirational book provokes questions about your current curriculum and provides plenty of guidance around how to transform your school's approach to teaching and learning. Jonathan Lear's monkey-proof box concept has been designed with children at the heart of every decision, and will undoubtedly inspire educators in all settings to take more risks.

A note of caution, however: Jonathan's innovative ideas may just have you swinging on your school playground's monkey bars!

Maxine Bradford, Head Teacher, Mildmay Infant and Nursery School

If you would like your pupils to get more enjoyment out of challenging tasks, then this is the book for you! *The Monkey-Proof Box* offers some lovely ideas for encouraging children to step out of their comfort zone, unleash their curiosity and apply their creative thinking.

The book's title comes from a scene in a nature documentary in which a group of monkeys were faced with a 'monkey-proof box', which prompted them to display a great degree of curiosity and creativity in order to extract the food from within it. And so it could be with pupils: not in terms of food perhaps, but certainly in terms of classroom culture. If we replace easy with engaging, straightforward with puzzling, and simple with stretching, then we could engage similar levels of innovation and determination in our learners. Imagine how productive that could be!

James Nottingham, creator of the Learning Pit

In *The Monkey-Proof Box* Jonathan Lear intertwines his unique combination of nostalgia, wit and first-class professional development insights to deliver a comprehensive concept of curriculum design. The book provides teachers and senior leaders alike with support and structure for planning and constructing a school's curriculum with children at its heart, and emphasises both a clear purpose and authenticity in what is learnt and what is produced. It also shares plenty of practical examples which will both challenge and inspire your pedagogical thinking.

Jonathan's personality and humour shine through in his writing as much as in real life, and this results in an easy-to-read book that will put a smile on your face and provide plenty of laugh-out-loud moments – texts such as this one are few and far between!

Daniel Callaghan, Head Teacher, Hartsholme Academy

Jonathan Lear

THE
MONKEY-PROOF
BOX

CURRICULUM design for building
KNOWLEDGE, developing **CREATIVE THINKING**
and promoting **INDEPENDENCE**

independent
thinking press

First published by
Independent Thinking Press
Crown Buildings, Bancyfelin, Carmarthen, Wales, SA33 5ND, UK
www.independentthinkingpress.com

and

Independent Thinking Press
PO Box 2223, Williston, VT 05495, USA
www.crownhousepublishing.com

Independent Thinking Press is an imprint of Crown House Publishing Ltd.

Cover image © Elly Walton, 2019.

Author photograph © Jane Hewitt, 2019.

Page 60, water cycle image © mervin07 – fotolia.com

Edited by Ian Gilbert

British Library of Cataloguing-in-Publication Data
A catalogue entry for this book is available from the British Library.

Print ISBN 978-178135310-3
Mobi ISBN 978-178135327-1
ePub ISBN 978-178135328-8
ePDF ISBN 978-178135329-5

LCCN 2019930244

Printed and bound in the UK by
TJ International, Padstow, Cornwall

For my amazing little boy, Reuben.

x

FOREWORD

Reading this book has been an uncanny experience for me.

It continually touches on areas that I have been fixated by and, when it does, it consistently enriches my thinking or helps to resolve my dilemmas. Like many people, particularly at the time of writing, I am fascinated by the idea of how we design and deliver the curriculum. We are increasingly told that the way in which we design our curriculum is the key to improving outcomes for young people, but that idea brings a huge number of challenges. Many of us have become more used to prescription than creativity. We are more used to meeting expectations than fulfilling ambitions when it comes to the curriculum. For many of us, curriculum design has become a lost art.

When we attempt to re-establish our skills, things can become even more fraught. We rarely encounter a curriculum that is genuinely deliverable. A brief examination of any GCSE, A level or any other certificate course usually reveals that it has far too much in it, and teachers edit the curriculum on the basis of their experience of the exams. We are very poor at deciding what to leave out.

We are also, as Jonathan points out, besieged by siren voices telling us that the curriculum must be overwhelmingly based on knowledge or that it must be defined by skills. The voices are always characterised by a resolute certainty and supported by an irresistible body of research. Unfortunately for schools – charged with developing a curriculum tailored to the needs of their specific communities and children, which must also be amenable to assessments that are nationally designed and acceptable to external inspectors – that resolute certainty exists on either side of the debate. There is also no shortage of research, since there seems to be more than enough to support both sides of the curriculum divide.

Jonathan deals with all of this brilliantly. He approaches the big questions about curriculum and pedagogy on the basis of realism, drawing on considerable experience and no small amount of humour. He can afford to do this because of the track record that he, and his school, has. The children with whom he works achieve well and that is recognised by secondary colleagues when they take on responsibility for them.

His track record is hugely important. We hear a great deal about 'evidence-based practice', usually as an encouragement to look at the practice of others, but we really need to draw on the evidence emerging from our own practice. Jonathan can do that with conviction and pride, and he deserves to be listened to because of the success that he achieves.

He is resolutely pragmatic. One of the endearing qualities of this book is something that I came to think of as 'warm cynicism'. Jonathan is not given to haughty, dismissive sarcasm, but he runs all ideas through a mill of common sense and experience, and not every idea makes it through.

These are qualities that we need. We need voices that are gentle, helpful and constructive. We need ideas that help us to develop our own thinking, and that we can take and apply. This book offers both the medium and the message.

I love Jonathan's emphasis on concepts and the useful examples of how to use them. I am equally impressed by his questions. His ideas are sound, but they are always validated by being tried and tested. Jonathan offers nothing that hasn't been put into practice and validated by impact. I wish that I had read this book much earlier in my career. There is so much of it that I would have used and so many hard lessons that I would not have needed to learn.

Alongside all of this, reading this book puts any reader into great company. Jonathan is funny. He is also open about his mistakes and willing to share them. There is no trace of pomposity. He writes as a father and a teacher. He invites you into his life and makes you very welcome indeed. That makes reading the book a particular pleasure. It manages to capture so much of the experience of hearing him speak. He is a superb presenter and trainer and that transfers joyously into the written word … And he quotes me! What more can I ask?

Now, step away from the foreword and start on the real treat.

(Real) David Cameron,
education consultant

CONTENTS

ACKNOWLEDGEMENTS

I would like to thank the incredible staff at St Catherine's Catholic Primary School for their positivity in trying new things and for thinking really hard about what they do and why; the brilliant people at Independent Thinking for their continued support, friendship and inspiration; all of the teachers, teaching assistants and leaders who have welcomed me into their schools over the past six years; and, most importantly, my amazing family – Emma, Eve, Imogen and Reuben – whose encouragement and support allows me to do the job that I love.

INTRODUCTION

I've worked at my school for twenty years now. I'm like an educational limpet – I've found a rock that I like and I'm staying put. This is because I'm happy. I love my school. I suppose that one of the reasons why I'm happy there is that it's such an interesting place. The children are amazing and form an incredibly diverse community. We're well above average in all sorts of things: pupil premium, FSM (free school meals), EAL (children whose first language isn't English), SEN (special educational needs, including those with an education, health and care plan), and we also sit in the top 5% in terms of the national school deprivation index.

It's exactly the kind of place I'd wanted to work in ever since I decided to become a teacher. When I first joined as a newly qualified teacher (NQT) things were a bit hairy. We were in some kind of category that was dished out to schools that weren't up to much. I didn't mind. In fact, I quite liked being called 'special'. Now we've been called 'outstanding'. We don't have a banner up and we haven't had t-shirts printed, but we're very proud of what our children achieve. They do brilliantly despite the challenges they face, and we're consistently told by the secondary schools they move up to that they're confident, articulate, independent and incredibly well prepared for the next stage in their education.

To get there, like all schools, we've had to work hard.

On a personal level, at the start of my career this meant trying to be the very best teacher I could be by doing as I was told. This didn't last long, and quite quickly an increasing aversion to some of the rubbish that we were being made to do by a government that didn't have a clue what they were up to led me into some small-scale militancy.

I decided that I couldn't keep up with the skip-full of new initiatives, programmes and support materials that were rolling into school on a weekly basis, so I decided to ignore them. I went back to my children uncluttered by the latest shiny educational invention. This wasn't laziness; I'd developed the attitude that if I didn't think it would improve things for the young people in front of me, I didn't bother with it. I got on with what I knew to be right, and as a result, the children in my class did very well.

I enjoyed being a bit militant. It was addictive. I started to think of myself as a guerrilla teacher – quietly undermining the immobile target that was the education system. I didn't get dressed up in camouflage or paint my face like someone from the SAS, but I did write a book about it.[1] I suppose I thought that if I talked about the stuff that went on in my classroom, then I could maybe chip away at some of nonsense that was happening around me.

That was when I was a classroom teacher. After accidentally falling into leadership, things changed. First of all, I realised that I didn't have to keep my approach to myself any more. I'd never shouted about my tactical ignoring before in case I got told off. With a new shiny deputy's badge, though, I was infinitely harder to sack. This instantly brought with it a new-found confidence and determination. I realised that rather than simply going guerrilla in my own classroom, I could now encourage others to behave in a similar way. Then I realised I could do it with an entire school.

This book is about what happens when you apply the same militant approach on a much bigger scale. I'd had enough of being told what to do and decided that there was another way – a different way. Designing a new curriculum is no mean feat, but if we really want something that's fit for purpose, then it's up to us – teachers, teaching assistants and leaders – to do it for ourselves.

---

1   J. Lear, *Guerrilla Teaching: Revolutionary Tactics for Teachers on the Ground, in Real Classrooms, Working with Real Children, Trying to Make a Real Difference* (Carmarthen: Independent Thinking Press, 2015).

Part I:
CURRICULUM

Chapter 1

Slippers

The idea of building a new curriculum didn't occur to me immediately. In fact, I didn't really think it was an option at all. There had always been plenty of documents close at hand to pick up and follow, so the thought of creating something new hadn't entered my head. Because of this, one of the first things I did was to have a look at what was already out there. There were, and are, quite a lot of curriculum packages floating around, but there wasn't anything that I thought would do the job. Schools are special places. They are part of a community, and whatever goes on in that school should bear some relation to this. A curriculum should be relevant – it should matter. Shipping in an off-the-shelf, ready-made package can be a solution, but it wasn't the solution for us.

The more I thought about this, the more I convinced myself that maybe building a curriculum from the ground up was the way to go. We were pretty confident that we knew what we wanted. As teachers, we'd grown up with the prescription of various different versions of the curriculum. We understood the need for rigour and wanted a curriculum model that was built on solid foundations. But more than this, we wanted it to be inspiring – the kind of curriculum that went beyond what we'd been used to in the past.

In a previous version of the national curriculum, teachers across the country were supported in delivering whatever it was we were supposed to be delivering thanks to some units written by the Qualifications and Curriculum Authority (QCA). These schemes were the epitome of functionality and included detailed plans for every subject. Coverage of content was ensured, and they were helpfully arranged into units that fitted neatly into a half-term. This usually meant that you had three geography units in a year, three history, three art, three design technology and so on. The mavericks amongst us decided to alternate one half-term of history with one of geography, one of art with one of design technology – just for the sheer excitement of it all. (See my top five QCA units on page 10.)

When it was all organised, we'd cut out the unit titles (using wooden letters – obviously) and stick them to our classroom display boards, so the children would know from day one exactly how rubbish their lives would be for the next six weeks. With this sorted, all that was left to do was deliver the units. This is where things started to go wrong because it turns out that six weeks isn't actually that long. This could just be the result of my failings as a teacher, but I never seemed to be anywhere near finishing a topic by the time half-term approached. This meant that the last week or so ended up in a mad rush to get stuff done because after the holiday I had to move onto something else.

Nowhere was this more apparent than with the most ill-conceived design technology topic ever created – 'Slippers'. To be honest, I've never fully understood slippers. I get what they're for, but they're not really the footwear of choice for your average revolutionary. I suppose I can accept that they have a place in society, for those who apparently can't bear to have their feet in contact with carpet, but no one will be able to convince me that they deserve a place in the curriculum.

'Slippers' was the actual name of a Year 6 unit – it wasn't dressed up as anything else and it wasn't even given one of the catchy titles that were dotted throughout the geography schemes (like 'Passport to the world' or, my personal favourite from Year 1, 'Where in the world is Barnaby Bear?'[1]

Regardless of my reservations, it had to be done because it said so in the scheme of work, and nobody really knew what would happen if we deviated from the plan.

'OK children – this half-term we're learning about slippers.'

Imagine saying that to a classroom full of children, and then imagine the reaction you might get. There were always one or two who seemed vaguely excited, but from the rest of them there was a collective sigh. I hate this as a teacher. In this sense, we're ultimately no different from a host of other performers – a dissatisfied response from the audience is like a dagger to the heart. To compensate, I decided to go heavy on the enthusiasm and proceeded to sell the topic to them like my life depended on it.

'Now, we're not just learning about slippers. We're actually going to make a pair ourselves …'

---

1 Barnaby was a teddy bear who travelled to different places around the world and brought back lots of photographs and artefacts to help the children learn more about that particular place. Admittedly, Barnaby's travels were essentially limited to wherever the teacher had booked for their half-term break. At best, this included highlights from a range of culturally enriching locations, and at worst, the children got to find out about the best bits of Magaluf.

A few more perked up at this point so I kept at it.

'We're going to design them ourselves – they might be fashion themed or sports themed or maybe like those furry animal/monster type ones – you know, the ones with the floppy ears and googly eyes. I've even seen some that squeak!'

They knew exactly what I meant, and thanks to my powers of persuasion, they were now absolutely buzzing. This was the start of my problems.

In hindsight, it's a terrible thing to raise children's expectations in the knowledge that something won't be as good as you've made out, but it was too late now. The children were already imagining skipping down to assembly and dazzling the rest of the school with their new footwear.

My first mistake was using the plural 'slippers'. The QCA scheme actually described the children producing a single slipper, or prototype, rather than a pair. I had missed this. Making one slipper makes even less sense than making two, but I couldn't worry about that now. We had sewing to do.

When I asked the children about their needlework skills, the last time they could remember sewing was when they were in nursery. And by sewing, what they really meant was stringing colourful shoelaces through a piece of wood with holes in it. I don't want to go into any more detail about what happened during the following six weeks, other than to say that I still have an overwhelming sense of dread at the merest mention of any textile-based craft activities.

The upshot was basically that neither I nor any of the kids had anything even approaching the kind of skill level necessary to pull off a pair of slippers. What they did produce was barely recognisable as a piece of footwear. There were soles formed from limp bits of cardboard with slices of rubber glued onto the bottom for grip. Some had managed the upper (a technical term we spoke about a lot without truly knowing what it meant) by stapling strips of hacked up fabric to their misshapen cardboard sole. Some still had the needles embedded in them because they had become so entangled that we felt it was probably best to leave them where they were. The children didn't wear their slippers to assembly. Instead, they remained on the windowsills of the classroom for the rest of the year as a constant reminder of just how inadequate we all were.

I gave myself a hard time over this kind of thing. Slippers is an extreme example, but I found that I was under pressure to get through similar stuff in most of the other subjects too. In the worst cases, it wasn't simply about not getting things done; sometimes, the children would really start getting into a topic, only for us to realise that it was week five and we only had another week left before we had to change to a new one. The whole business was frustrating, but we kept at it because that's what it said on the plan.

This exemplifies one of the problems with being a teacher. Most of us do stuff because we're told to do it, and then when it doesn't work or becomes unmanageable we blame ourselves, feel guilty about it all and pretend that everything is fine whenever anybody asks. Most of us don't like to feel that we're letting anyone else down so we don't talk about it. This is such a damaging thing to do, yet it's incredibly common – mainly due to the fact that we really care about what we do and desperately want to do the best we can for our children.

I knew there were topics that weren't particularly worthwhile. I also knew that I was constantly chasing my tail because I couldn't fit everything in. I had a sneaking suspicion that the four weeks we had spent gluing screwed up newspaper balls together to make a volcano were probably a waste of time, and that lots of the work I'd got them to record in their books as evidence didn't actually mean much in the long run. In short, I had the feeling that I was rubbish at my job.

So I decided to say it. I found a friendly and more experienced colleague who I knew wouldn't judge me too harshly and told them everything. I was expecting a bit of sympathy and hopefully some advice. What I got was a bit unexpected. She said, 'I know what you mean – I think that too.'

It was a bit of a moment – we hugged and there were tears, then we got a cuppa and started to talk about all of the things that we couldn't do or couldn't cope with. Admitting it, and finding someone who struggled in exactly the same way, was like a weight being lifted, and now that there were two of us, we were almost certain that there must be more.

There were. In fact, virtually the whole staff was feeling incompetent – it was brilliant. None of us could do our jobs as well as we wanted, and we'd never been happier.

There's an important lesson in here for experienced teachers. I think we sometimes do a disservice to young teachers who are coming into the profession. We might end up as mentors, coaches or respected elders, but how often do we speak openly about our struggles – the things we find hard, the things we know we don't do well or have the time to do well? I'm not advocating the celebration of mediocrity, but I do think that the efficiency and levels of automaticity that we've developed over time must seem almost superhuman to teachers at the beginning of their careers. We've got to show our cracks (you know what I mean).

So, back to being incompetent. This collective acceptance that things weren't working ultimately led to one of the best decisions we made as a school. We were all trying to do everything. If it was written in a curriculum document or appeared in a scheme of work, we would cover it. As a result, the outcomes for the children were hit and miss. Some of their work was good, and some of it wasn't. It was incredibly rare, however, to be able to describe any of their work as genuinely brilliant.

Any curriculum document is designed to be both practical and useful – the definition of functional. To make it beautiful as well means making some decisions, compromises even, to make sure we get the balance right.

We wanted our children to have the opportunity to produce incredible work – to be exposed to a world beyond slippers. And for this to happen, we had to accept that we would need to do less, but do it better.

My top five inspirational QCA units

1. **Containers:** A Year 5 art and design topic during which the children spent six weeks inventing a thing that holds some other things – basically a box.

2. **Biscuits:** Design technology this time. If spending six weeks on a biscuit wasn't exciting enough, we were encouraged to jazz it up by making it 'cultural'.

3. **Local traffic:** Geography, apparently.

4. **Controlling a turtle:** A classic from Year 2. This was ICT before proper technology had been invented and was based around using 'Roamer' – a programmable bin lid that could go forwards, backwards and occasionally around a corner. The turtle effect was achieved by gluing an egg box onto its back, although I got told off by the ICT coordinator for 'making a mockery of the technology'.

5. **Rock and soils:** The title of this Year 3 unit should be enough to put most people off, but I have met some budding geologists who really liked teaching it. These people are not normal and should be avoided.

Chapter 2

LESS IS MORE

Doing less, but doing it better, seems like a completely obvious and straightforward thing to do, but actually it's quite complicated. In any curriculum document, the stuff that's included is in there because someone has decided that it's clearly very important. Whether it's framed as 'essential knowledge', 'core knowledge' or something else, this can be contentious – mainly due to the issue of who's done the deciding in the first place.

I'm occasionally approached by teachers of a certain age who like to tell me what it was like in the pre-curriculum 'good old days' when they had almost complete control over content. They would happily make up topics about whatever they wanted – never knowing from one day to the next where the wind would take them. They describe children who were captivated by a topic on squirrels – a subject plucked out of thin air just because the teacher happened to see one on their way to work. However, having a working knowledge of squirrels doesn't make up for the fact that your pupils are virtually illiterate and unable to count past ten. The good old days didn't really exist, and whilst schools were busy teaching whatever they liked, there were children up and down the country experiencing a completely inconsistent education. You could view the introduction of a standardised curriculum as a necessary evil, but something had to happen to tighten things up – it's just that it's gone too far.

Now, as much as I don't want everyone simply making stuff up, I'm equally against some central body or organisation having complete control over what the children in my school should learn about. I want a middle ground. I don't mind that we have curriculum documents, but they need to be viewed as a framework – a starting point rather than a set of instructions to be slavishly followed.

I was listening recently to my favourite Scottish person, the education guru and author of the foreword to this book, David Cameron, who described successful schools as being those that 'adapt' rather than 'adopt'. I really like this. Historically, there's been way too much adopting going on in schools, without addressing what is probably the most important question of all: what is it our children need? It's a tough one this, and there are no easy answers. What seems obvious, though, is that this is a question that is best answered by schools rather than by anyone else.

Committing to doing less means that, along with adapting whatever we've got in front of us, we also need a healthy dose of ignoring. We'll look at the decision-making process around this particular aspect of militancy in Chapter 5, but before we do, it's worth clearing up some of the confusion about what the curriculum is (or what it should be) in the first place.

Depending on who you're listening to, it seems that a curriculum should be either knowledge based or skills based. This is the first thing we need to get our heads around, mainly to save ourselves the frustration of going round in pointless circles instead of focusing on the things that actually matter.

I don't want to get into the whole knowledge versus skills debate – largely because I think viewing these two things as separate entities is a waste of time. Most teachers I've come across would agree that knowledge and skills are intrinsically linked, but it's probably closer to the truth to view skills as a particular type of knowledge. For example, when I say that I *know* how to ride a bike, I'm not talking about just knowing the theory – I mean that I've got the skills needed to do it.[1]

This is a bit complicated because we're talking about two different types of knowledge: propositional knowledge (knowing facts) and procedural knowledge (knowing how to do things). Traditionally, we've used the terms 'knowledge' and 'skills' to distinguish between the two, and for the sake of keeping everything nice and clear, I don't see any reason why this should change. It's not either/or – any curriculum worth its salt needs both. Knowing stuff is really important, but I want this to happen in a way that also allows children to develop skills. This boils down to the 'what' and the 'how' of what we do, and understanding how to deal with these two concepts is a key part of creating the balanced curriculum that we're after.

---

1 For an introduction on how philosophers approach knowledge see G. Henriques, What Is Knowledge? A Brief Primer, *Psychology Today* (4 December 2013). Available at: https://www.psychologytoday.com/intl/blog/theory-knowledge/201312/what-is-knowledge-brief-primer.

Chapter 3
SKILLS

There are two distinct groups of skills within the context of a curriculum. The first are those generic skills that would apply to pretty much all areas of learning, and the second are those that could be categorised as subject-specific skills.

The generic 'learning and thinking' skills are the ones that people seem to get most fired up about. They're also the ones that seem to have spurred mini industries into knocking out different coloured thinking hats or puppets called 'Ricky Resourcefulness' or (my personal favourite) 'Rhiannon Reciprocity'.

To start with, I don't think any child ever became more resourceful by sitting in an assembly listening to a story about a puppet who dealt skilfully with an unforeseen set of circumstances. I've even got a feeling that as a young teacher I was made to take part in such a scenario, as the character 'Robbie Resilient', to teach the unsuspecting children an important life lesson about perseverance. It's a very vague memory because I've tried to blank it out.

The reason this doesn't work is not because the idea is wrong or even that the learning and thinking skills we're attempting to develop aren't valuable. It's because the application of them is often a superficial attempt to add these skills as a quick fix on top of an existing curriculum model. If this is the case, you can have all the displays you like about resilience, resourcefulness and reciprocity, but it won't make the slightest bit of difference if there isn't the opportunity for the children to develop and practise them.

These kinds of skills should be the by-product of a curriculum, and so before building a curriculum that aims to achieve this goal, it's a good idea to clarify what we're hoping to achieve. Fortunately, rather than having to reinvent the wheel, there are places to go for exactly this kind of information.

My first port of call was to go back to a document called 'A Framework of Personal, Learning and Thinking Skills' that was originally created by the QCA.[1]

---

1   Qualifications and Curriculum Authority, A Framework of Personal, Learning and Thinking Skills (2011). Available at: http://webarchive.nationalarchives.gov.uk/20110215111658/http://curriculum.qcda. gov.uk/key-stages-3-and-4/skills/personal-learning-and-thinking-skills/index.aspx.

It was targeted at children aged eleven to nineteen and comprises of six groups of skills which, along with English, mathematics and ICT, are 'essential to success in learning, life and work'.

Ignoring the fact that it was really aimed at children older than primary age, the first step we took was to pick out the kinds of skills we wanted to emerge as a result of every aspect of our curriculum.

Basic skills

- To speak clearly and convey ideas confidently.
- To read and to communicate ideas in writing efficiently and effectively.
- To calculate efficiently and apply skills to solve problems.
- To use new technologies confidently and purposefully.

Active learning

- To seek out and enjoy challenges.
- To collaborate with others.
- To show commitment and perseverance.
- To assess themselves and others.

Creative thinking

- To ask questions to extend thinking.
- To generate ideas and explore possibilities.
- To overcome barriers by trying out alternatives and adapting or developing ideas.
- To connect ideas and experiences in inventive ways.

The basic skills bit wouldn't be classed as learning and thinking skills at all – it's the main focus of what we do in schools and you would struggle to find anyone who didn't value it as an outcome. However, active learning and creative thinking definitely fall into the generic skills category.

If we didn't have a curriculum that developed the basic skills then it would be fair to say that we were failing our children. I think it's also reasonable to suggest that the curriculum would be a failure if it didn't also instil a desire to learn by producing children who 'seek out and enjoy challenges'. You could say exactly the same thing about collaboration or perseverance, and you can definitely say the same thing about creative thinking.

Every aspect of creative thinking is about being an effective learner, and you're not an effective learner if you can only do it when you're in school and being told what to do. I'm not a fan of phrases like 'lifelong learner' but this is exactly what we're talking about, and it's exactly what the world beyond school is looking for. We all want young people to be literate, numerate and technologically capable, but we also need young people who can think for themselves.

Beyond these three aims, the other skills we were interested in were then organised thanks to our first key decision: to achieve a slimmed down, 'less is more' curriculum, we stopped working in six-week, half-termly blocks and started working across an entire term. This instantly provided the opportunity to do things properly for a change, and to prevent us from falling back into a pattern of trying to squeeze everything in, we identified key areas of the curriculum that we would only teach once in the year. In history, geography, the arts subjects and design technology, each year group would learn about just one topic; we would work on the topic for a term and do it exceptionally well.

In terms of structure, we gave each term a specific focus. Our autumn term was named 'Discover' and was history themed; the spring term, 'Explore', had a geography and design technology focus; and the summer term, 'Create', was arts themed.

With the overall structure sorted, we could map the remaining skills to the terms in which it felt most appropriate:

Discover
(history themed)

- Identify questions to answer and problems to solve.
- Plan and research.
- Analyse and evaluate.
- Show empathy.
- Show a commitment to justice.
- Explore issues, events and problems from different perspectives.
- Support conclusions using reasoned arguments and evidence.
- Communicate learning in relevant ways.

Explore
(geography and design technology themed)

- Identify questions to answer and problems to solve.
- Recognise that pupils can impact their environment and community.
- Show a commitment to justice.
- Recognise pupils' role as global citizens.
- Communicate learning in relevant ways.
- Show empathy.

Create
(arts themed)

- Identify questions to answer and problems to solve.
- Show flexibility.
- Organise time and resources.
- Communicate the learning in relevant ways.
- Work towards a goal.
- Adapt ideas as circumstances change.
- Show empathy.

Some of the skills are repeated across the terms – for example, 'Show empathy' and 'Identify questions to answer and problems to solve' feature in all three terms. This is based on the fact that we shouldn't be teaching history, geography, design technology or art without also aiming to develop empathy, and if we're interested in developing independence and curiosity, then a good place to start is by encouraging the children to identify and ask questions. The same could be said for 'communicate the learning in relevant ways' – it's a constant (or it should be), so it's in there to give it the importance it deserves.

Whilst it's impossible to identify exactly what is needed in order to live a successful life, there's no question that these skills are desirable. I'm not interested in a curriculum that explicitly teaches children how to 'overcome barriers', 'make connections', 'show flexibility' or any of the other skills listed, but I am interested in a curriculum that creates the conditions for these skills to develop – and instead of sitting around and debating their relative merits, we're much better off spending our time thinking about how we might make it happen.

Chapter 4

TIGHTROPE WALKING

Having a fancy structure and neat lists of skills is all well and good, but we're edging pretty close to some kind of weird commune where we all just float around collaborating with our fellow global citizens. For a curriculum to be effective, it needs rigour – and for that, we need something concrete from which to build.

Along with the learning and thinking skills, we've also got subject-specific skills to contend with. These skills are an essential part of the work we do with our children; again, if we're not extremely careful, they're really easy to miss. Quite often in curriculum documents, the subject-specific skills are either not made explicit or, worse, they're buried under the weight of content that has to be delivered.

Making the decision to approach the content of the curriculum with much more flexibility meant that having a clear approach to the development of these subject-specific skills became essential. First up, we had to find them. In the olden days, we used to have a skills document. This usually took the form of a series of grids that outlined exactly what skills our children would need to develop in order to be scientists, historians, geographers, designers and so on.

In history, for example, the skills we want the children to develop are applicable to any time period they are exloring, such as 'Recognise and interpret primary and secondary sources' (Year 6). This is an enquiry skill, and having a clear understanding of how this can be broken down and developed across each year group is incredibly helpful.

Let's start with the following objective: *We are learning about Roman political life*. There's nothing necessarily wrong with this, but if we use it as it stands we're limiting our options. If we're doing the Romans, then knowing about Roman political life is important. If we're interested in being more sophisticated in our approach than just telling the pupils what they need to know, then we can view the knowledge as the outcome, rather than the learning.

Here's where knowledge and skills become intertwined. We want the children to know about the Romans (or Roman political life), but we also want them to learn about it whilst developing a useful skill (the 'what' and the 'how' we looked at earlier), so: *We are learning to* recognise and interpret primary sources *to help us find out about Roman political life.* We can't learn, develop or practise this skill without applying it to a piece of knowledge, and if we attempt to teach children the knowledge without bothering with the skill, then we're reducing history, or anything else for that matter, to nothing more than a body of facts to be remembered.

Using existing documents and anything else we could find, it didn't take long to create skills progression grids across the whole curriculum. They started at Year 1 and clearly demonstrated the development of skills through to Year 6. To make the progression as clear as possible, we weren't just interested in what this would look like from one year group to the next; we also wanted to know what progression would look like within a year group. To help with this we used the SOLO taxonomy.

SOLO stands for Structure of Observed Learning Outcomes and is a model that describes levels of increasing complexity in understanding. It was devised by John Biggs and Kevin Collis in the 1980s and has been used in various different ways since then.[1] It became quite popular a few years ago with lots of secondary teachers as a means of making the process of learning more explicit within lessons, but then seemed to fall out of favour pretty quickly following the realisation that the time spent getting the children to understand the various stages might be better spent just teaching them important stuff.

Despite the criticism, I've always believed that it's not necessarily what you've got but what you do with it that counts, and whilst I'm not particularly interested in spending time teaching the stages of the taxonomy to the children, it does have an extremely useful application in terms of supporting the structure of skills progression.

---

1   J. Biggs and K. Collis, *Evaluating the Quality of Learning: The SOLO Taxonomy* (New York: Academic Press, 1982).

The taxonomy breaks down learning into five levels:[2]

Prestructural: The pupil hasn't fully understood the point and can only give a very basic response.

Unistructural: The pupil's response focuses on just one relevant aspect.

Multistructural: The pupil's response focuses on several relevant aspects.

Relational: The different aspects have become integrated into a coherent whole.

Extended abstract: The whole may become conceptualised at a higher level of abstraction and generalised to a new topic or area.

This all sounds very clever. Quite often this is not a good thing – there is a lot to be said for keeping everything as straightforward as possible. In this case, though, I think the cleverness translates very well into something that is of practical use – the beginnings of a clear focus for curriculum planning.

If we take the Year 6 skill we looked at above, 'recognise and interpret primary sources', there's the risk that, even if we do make it our focus, it could still fall victim to being 'covered' and ticked off. We'll explore the process of learning in Part II, but one of the most important shifts in our collective thinking as teachers has been in our understanding that learning happens over time rather than in a single lesson. We could just return to the objective and repeat it over the course of the topic. This would help with the learning (and the retention of learning) side of things, but not so much with the children's depth of understanding. For this, we need the helpful set of verbs that come with each SOLO level.

The three levels that we were most interested in were multistructural, relational and extended abstract. I don't fully understand why prestructural exists as a level – maybe it's for the sake of completion, but I don't think there will be many teachers out there who aim for children to be happily tootling along in blissful ignorance. I feel the same about unistructural. If we've decided to work across a whole term, then we can't (and definitely shouldn't) get away with the children just knowing or being able to do a few things. If we're aiming for greater depth, it's got to be our intention to build a significant body of knowledge and skills. We need to make the most out of the space and time we've got.

---

2   See http://www.johnbiggs.com.au/academic/solo-taxonomy/.

The SOLO taxonomy only really gets going when we hit the multistructural stage, where the pupils' responses focus on several (ideally lots) of relevant aspects. This felt like a decent entry point for building the 'in-year' progression we were after. After some experimentation, here's what it looked like for the history skill we considered earlier:

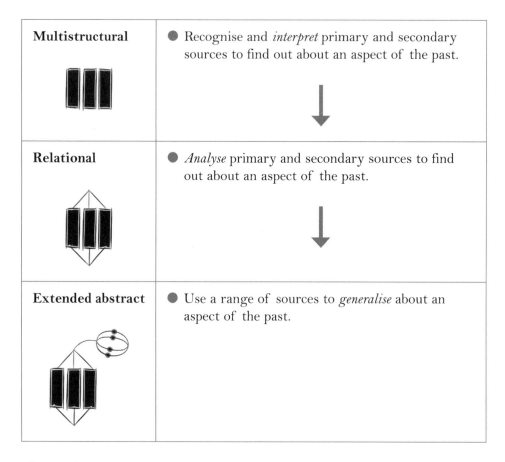

Multistructural	Recognise and *interpret* primary and secondary sources to find out about an aspect of the past.
Relational	*Analyse* primary and secondary sources to find out about an aspect of the past.
Extended abstract	Use a range of sources to *generalise* about an aspect of the past.

There's definite progression here. As a teacher, you've got somewhere to go with it all. It also helps with sequencing. Imagine jumping in and attempting to teach children how to generalise as a skill without having made sure that there was a significant body of knowledge in place first. It wouldn't make any sense. Generalise sits where it does for a reason. Interpret (making sense of the words within the historical source – understanding the content) and analyse (looking at the source methodically and in detail) both allow the children to build knowledge. When we're happy that this has happened, then we can think about skills like generalising.

Another point worth noting is that whilst there are three boxes above, this doesn't equate to three lessons. Furthermore, whilst the taxonomy might represent increasing complexity, it definitely doesn't represent a hierarchy of importance. The skills of interpreting and analysing are every bit as important as generalising, and we might actually spend quite a lot of time on the first two before looking at developing anything else. Regardless of how long we might spend working on each aspect, the overall aim should be for all the children to have an opportunity to work at the extended abstract stage.

Along with the obvious benefits for our children, this does an important job for us too. Having a solid foundation gives you confidence, and it's much easier to take risks (and to justify them) if you know you've got something backing you up. At some point, if you do decide to do things differently, you'll find yourself in a situation in which someone will ask you what you're up to and why. And when the questions come, you need to be able to look them squarely in the eye and let them have it:

Our curriculum is skills based and knowledge rich; we cover less because we believe that our children should have the opportunity to study areas of the curriculum in greater depth. We want our children to produce exceptional outcomes whilst developing their independence, curiosity and creativity. We want to produce collaborators, innovators, leaders and, more than anything else, young people who understand what it means to be human.

Perfect. Now all we've got to do is put it into practice.

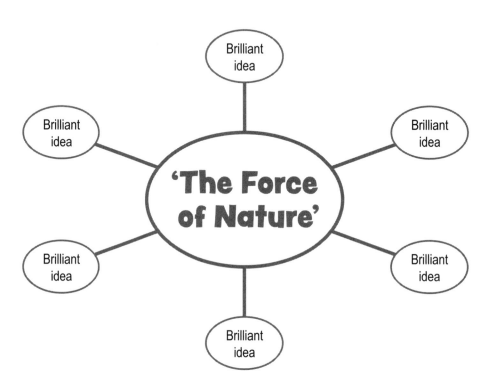

Chapter 5

PLANNING

With skills-based non-negotiables underpinning the curriculum, we've now got the platform we need to start thinking about how we deal with the content.

I've always secretly liked planning. I've never admitted this before because I think it's probably one of the things that we're expected to feel deeply unhappy about as teachers, but I've always found planning – and, in particular, the planning of topics – to be a pretty exciting business. I think it's because it's a chance to be creative and come up with brilliant things to do with the children, and when it's done, you get the warm glow that comes from having created something interesting, exciting and new.

The process relies heavily on us taking advantage of our ability to make connections based on our knowledge of the curriculum for our year group. One way to approach this is to come up with broad topic names that enable us to fit in everything we want to cover. Because of the three-term structure, the main focus for each of our topics was either history, geography or art, with the intention that as many other curriculum areas as possible would be woven in along the way.

For example, let's take a topic called 'The Force of Nature'. Right from the outset, it seems to have more going on than some of the QCA offerings we looked at earlier. As a highly creative teacher, you've probably already come up with various different aspects of the curriculum that you would include under this title before I've even got to the end of this sentence.

If that is you, then you're probably now reaching for a sheet of paper to start your spider diagram/topic web/mind-map. You might even be using different colour gel pens. Us creative types love a spider diagram. If you're unfamiliar with this particular subgenre of planning, it looks a bit like the figure on page 24.

I know it doesn't have the right number of legs for an actual spider, but we can gloss over that for now. Sometimes it might have just four circles around the outside, sometimes six or seven; it all depends on how many different subject areas we've cleverly connected to the topic name.

If we start with geography, we'd be looking at earthquakes, natural disasters and volcanic eruptions. In science, a natural fit would be forces or reversible and irreversible changes. In English, it could be narrative – adventure/survival stories or non-chronological reports. We could also throw in some journalistic writing about a natural disaster, or maybe first-person diary entries from people who witnessed the eruption/earthquake/tsunami for themselves. It might be a geography-themed topic, but we could sprinkle in a bit of history too – maybe Pompeii or some other relevant historical event. In art, there are some great starting points for exploring the force of nature – there's Katsushika Hokusai's famous print, *The Great Wave*, or the photograph *Lighthouse in a Storm* by Jean Guichard. I don't need to go on any more because you've already thought of most of these yourself, along with others that I haven't mentioned and possibly haven't even thought about. This is the joy of working creatively as a teacher – the ideas start to flow and we get carried away. Before we know it, we've got enough going on to last the entire year and possibly beyond.

But before we get too caught up in our own brilliance, it's worth considering that things might not be as rosy as they appear. First of all, it's important to say that there's nothing terribly wrong with planning in this way – the children definitely benefit. But if we take a step back, there's no getting away from the fact that it's us being creative, rather than them. If we genuinely value creative thinking as something we want young people to develop, then this doesn't sit right. Traditional topic planning is driven by teachers: we come up with the ideas, we make the connections, we usually decide exactly what the outcomes will look like. A well-designed topic will engage and motivate the children. They will enjoy it. But if we want more than this, then we'll need to approach it from a different angle.

Along with the problem of teachers dominating the whole process, there's also the issue of *how* we're making the connections. Topic planning is essentially about finding cross-curricular links. The search for these links had become so prominent in schools that we often had special boxes on our planning sheets to make sure that we didn't forget to do it. This brought out the worst in some of us, and the desire to be creative took on a slightly competitive edge, with the determination to create as many cross-curricular links as was humanly possible. This led to some quite unexpected and improbable combinations – my old design technology nemesis 'Slippers' suddenly found itself linked to music, for the obvious reason that slippers are usually worn by old people who also like listening to classical music. This kind of link wasn't uncommon. It didn't really matter how tenuous the connection was – if there was the tiniest thread that might connect two subjects, we went for it.

I think part of the problem here is in the name. Cross-curricular links do exactly what you expect them to do – make connections within and between different aspects of the curriculum. In the grand scheme of things, the curriculum is actually quite a small box. Outside of the box we have the world, and there are some pretty big things in it. Reducing ourselves to only ever making connections within the curriculum seems to be ignoring some much more important, and potentially more interesting, connections that could emerge if we stopped to consider the bigger picture.

To help us get to the big stuff, a useful starting point is the idea of concepts. Concepts are the things that float around in our heads and inform our thoughts, beliefs and most aspects of our thinking – things like 'justice', 'free will', 'truth', 'democracy' and 'friendship'.

Concepts don't fall into subject boxes, and they don't tend to appear in any curriculum documents. They do, however, give us the opportunity to create the connectedness we're after by lifting us above the content we should be teaching to a position where we can start to see things from a wider perspective. Along with this, concepts can help us to tap into the personal learning and thinking skills. Developing 'empathy', discovering a 'commitment to justice' or enabling children to recognise that they can have an impact on their 'environment and community' won't happen with us delivering the curriculum, but it can happen if we filter the content through concepts.

Beyond providing meaning, identifying concepts also enables us to develop connections that extend further than the topic the children happen to be working on. This isn't necessarily a given in terms of how the brains of young people work. For lots of children, the Ancient Greeks topic they did in Year 3 is completely different and separate to the Romans in Year 4, and different again to the Second World War in Year 6. The only thing that ties them together is the fact that it's called 'history'.

If, however, we identified the concept of 'democracy', we've suddenly got a way to join up the dots:

- Ancient Greece: Athenian democracy – 'demokratia' and the beginnings of people power.
- Romans: The Republic – consuls, senators and the Plebeian Council.
- The Second World War: The rise of Hitler and the Nazi Party – from democracy to dictatorship.

Using concepts in this way means that, along with themes that link *within* a subject, we can also make connections *across* subjects and, beyond subjects, across traditional topics. For example, 'human rights', 'justice', 'beauty' and 'equality' are all concepts that could be explored and revisited through history, geography, science and art. By taking a broader view of things, we can get to some pretty big ideas and, as a happy by-product, also reposition two subjects that have a history of being pushed to the edges.

I probably shouldn't admit to this, but one of the two areas that frequently takes a back seat in the topic-building stakes is religious education. We all teach RE, and as a Catholic school it's an important part of what we do. One of the things we found, though, was that it frequently sat on the fringes of the topics. The other subjects would link up really nicely, but RE was a sticking point. As a result, on lots of occasions it was taught separately and frequently squeezed into gaps in the timetable, somewhere between English, maths and PE. The other area that often suffers a similar fate is personal, social, health and economic (PSHE) education. It can be a tough one to shoehorn into a topic and so it's usually left on its own – it might get an hour on the timetable or be delivered in weekly circle time.

In terms of the aims of these two subjects, there's actually a very good argument to suggest that they might be amongst the most important things the children will ever learn about. In Sheffield, the Standing Advisory Council on Religious Education (SACRE) have created their own RE syllabus called *Enquiring Minds & Open Hearts* which, had I thought of it first, would probably have made a much better title for this book. In the document, they describe the purpose of RE as follows:

Religious education in Sheffield schools contributes dynamically to children and young people's education in schools, provoking challenging questions about human life, beliefs, communities and ideas. In RE pupils learn from religions and world views about different ways of life in local, national and global contexts. They discover, explore and consider many different answers to questions about human identity, meaning and value. They learn to weigh up for themselves the value of wisdom from different communities, to disagree respectfully, to be reasonable in their responses to religions and world views and to respond by express [*sic*] insights into their own and others' lives. They are encouraged to develop enquiring minds, and to think rigorously, creatively, imaginatively and respectfully about their ideas in relation to religions and world views.[1]

There's a lot to like about this, but the thing that jumps out the most is that this is clearly linked to the idea of developing concepts.

PSHE can be viewed in exactly the same way. In the PSHE Association's *Programme of Study for PSHE Education (Key Stages 1–5)*, the concepts are there in black and white: 'identity', 'relationships', risk', 'diversity and equality', 'rights', 'responsibility', 'consent', 'change', 'resilience' and 'power'.[2] If we start by identifying the concepts that can be explored through curriculum content, then RE and PSHE suddenly become central.

A useful way to approach this is to have the different elements of the curriculum laid out in front of you (literally, if it helps). With an overview of the content we need/want to cover, we can pick out the main subject focus for a particular project. For example, if we settle on history, instead of immediately looking across the curriculum for other subjects to link to it, we can look for connecting concepts.

The grid on page 30 is not meant to be a comprehensive list, but it's not a bad starting point.

If the period in history we're looking at is Britain in the 1900s, and specifically the history of the *Titanic*, then based on what we know, we might pick out the

---

1 Sheffield SACRE, *Enquiring Minds & Open Hearts: Religious Education for All. The Agreed Syllabus for RE in Sheffield 2014–2019*. Available at: http://www.learnsheffield.co.uk/Downloads/Partnerships/SACRE%20 Agreed%20Syllabus%202014%20-%202019.pdf, p. 4.

2 PSHE Association, *Programme of Study for PSHE Education (Key Stages 1–5)* (London: PSHE Association, 2017). Available at: https://www.pshe-association.org.uk/system/files/PSHE%20Education%20 Programme%20of%20Study%20%28Key%20stage%201-5%29%20Jan%202017_2.pdf.

Adversity	Consequences	Freedom	Passion	Spirituality
Beauty	Creativity	Friendship	Peace	Stewardship
Belief	Democracy	Happiness	Poverty	Strength
Belonging	Discrimination	Identity	Power	Sustainability
Care	Diversity	Individuality	Prejudice	Tradition
Change	Dreams	Influence	Pride	Transformation
Choice	Duty	Integration	Protest	Trust
Class	Equality	Judgement	Reform	Truth
Cohesion	Failure	Justice	Resilience	Value
Common good	Fairness	Love	Responsibility	Virtue
Community	Faith	Loyalty	Rights	Weakness
Compassion	Fear	Media	Sacrifice	Wealth
Conflict	Forgiveness	Morality	Segregation	Well-being
Consent	Free will	Oppression	Service	Wisdom

Concept grid

concepts of 'class', 'segregation', 'fairness' and 'oppression'. The ability to do this effectively is totally dependent on how well we know the particular period we've picked, but hopefully we wouldn't consider going for something like the *Titanic* unless our subject knowledge is up to scratch. If it isn't, we end up focusing too much on details and we miss the bigger themes.

Concepts:
Class, segregation, fairness, oppression

History: Britain in the 1900s – *RMS Titanic*

Connection to concepts:

Tickets were divided into three classes based on wealth and social class – the starting point for exploring the *Titanic* as a microcosm of Edwardian society.

Being able to identify the concept of class automatically gives the history of the *Titanic* a much more interesting and powerful angle, and, as a result, allows us to make broader connections to RE and PSHE.[3]

---

3 PSHE Association, *Programme of Study for PSHE Education*: core theme 3 – 'Living in the wider world'.

Concepts:

Class, segregation, fairness, oppression

History: Britain in the 1900s – *RMS Titanic*	PSHE: Living in the wider world	RE: The common good
Connection to concepts:	Connection to concepts:	Connection to concepts:
Tickets were divided into three classes based on wealth and social class – the starting point for exploring the *Titanic* as a microcosm of Edwardian society.	Human rights, discrimination of individuals and communities, national, regional, religious and ethnic identities.	Kindness, unselfishness, a commitment to justice, community cohesion and the importance of rights and responsibilities.

We could go further by adding more curriculum areas. Some, like RE and PSHE, might be given the same time and attention as our main subject focus (history), and others might be dipped into or form just a small part of the overall project. A good example of this would be the arts. When we considered the structure of the curriculum earlier, the arts had their own dedicated term – 'create'. This is because art, music, dance and drama should have as much importance as anything else in the curriculum and they deserve to be taught properly. This doesn't mean that there won't be the opportunity to use the arts throughout the rest of the year too.

To differentiate between when a particular subject is the main focus and when it was being added alongside something else, we used the terms 'focus' and 'enhancement'. It might be that the main focus of the autumn term was history, but it could have an arts enhancement that would enrich the learning. In this example, rather than just defaulting to making paintings of the *Titanic* or creating a model of an iceberg, we might explore the concepts of class or oppression by listening to and interpreting protest music or by looking at the work of L. S. Lowry. In terms of the enhancement being purposeful, even though it may only constitute a small part of the project, we ensure that it's done well by going back to the subject-specific skills progression grids for art (or whichever subject we're interested in) and finding an appropriate skill that we could develop.

The same could be said for any other subject. If the main focus of the spring term was geography, but there happened to be an element of history that would enhance things, then rather than ignore it, we would add it in – as long as it didn't distract us from the clarity of our main focus or take us away from our 'less is more' philosophy. In each case, whether we're dealing with a focus subject or an enhancement, we're applying the same thinking: it's not about linking subjects with each other but about finding the concepts that allow us to thread everything together.[4]

This concept-based learning approach is a great way to create a cohesive and joined up curriculum, but it's not quite classroom-ready yet. To help prevent us slipping back into our old topic-building, teacher-dominated ways, we decided to banish the term 'topic' for good. Instead, we started to use the term 'project' – for no other reason than it sounded more like a thing we'd do together with the children, rather than something that gets delivered at them.

This 'togetherness' – and with it the opportunity for the children to have some input into the process – was then reinforced by beginning with a question. Starting with an enquiry question that frames the concepts we're interested in means that right from the outset, the children have got a focus. If we think about the previous example, we'd picked Britain in the 1900s as our content and identified 'class', 'segregation', 'fairness' and 'oppression' as the concepts. The enquiry question that frames the concepts, and becomes our starting point for the project, could be along the lines of: 'Should we accept our place in society?'

In terms of question design, we've definitely gone a bit philosophical here, rather than a more literal, 'What was society like in Edwardian times?' This is a very

---

4 A happy by-product of this approach is that it's also much easier to identify high quality books to enhance the work that we're doing. We don't have to find a novel that's specifically about the *Titanic* or even about Edwardian England; we're after something that ties into the concepts we're exploring instead. This opens things up to a much greater selection of titles, and also reduces the chances of us making do with some dodgy bit of writing just because it fits with a topic on the Egyptians or rivers.

deliberate choice and is partly to do with helping to create a connection or relevance to the children's lives (as opposed to it just being about some people who lived a long time ago), but mainly to keep things as open and divergent as possible.

There's an argument that because the enquiry question is written by the teacher, it's no different to them making up a topic name – neither approach involves the children. The difference becomes apparent with what happens next. Once you've shared a topic name with the children, you usually just get on with it.[5] But a question, especially a philosophical one, has the effect of generating more questions. It can't be answered immediately because the children don't know enough about it yet, so it has to be unpicked. This process then allows us to explore the concepts and kick-start the children's curiosity and desire to find out more, with the opportunity for them to develop further lines of enquiry.

In a Year 6 geography-themed project that explored the concepts of 'change', 'resilience', 'well-being' and 'equality', the children looked at the impact of natural disasters in different parts of the world. Before getting into the geography curriculum content, they started to think about the concepts by responding to the question, 'Does adversity always make you stronger?' Again, as well as creating the opportunity to draw in aspects of RE, PSHE or any other curriculum areas the teachers were interested in, the enquiry question was also the spark for the children's own incredibly powerful thoughts (see page 35).

There's definitely important stuff going on here – the kind of questions that children don't get to ask often enough. Some tie in directly to the concepts we're interested in – for example, 'Does adversity affect people in different ways?' would allow us to explore resilience and well-being. Other questions seem to be heading in a slightly different direction: 'If there is a God, how come terrible things happen in the world?' or 'What is the point of prayer?' These both fit much better with the concept of 'faith' – not something that was necessarily identified in the planning of the project but could be woven in now that the questions have been asked.

---

5   Sometimes we'd convince ourselves that the children were actually having an input into the topic by completing something called a KWL grid. This little activity allowed us to get a feel for what the children already knew (K), what they wanted to know (W) and, at the end of it all, what they'd learnt (L). The problem was that we'd already planned the topic by this point, so as soon as they'd filled in the boxes on the sheet, we'd tuck it away and get on with doing exactly what we'd come up with in the first place.

What is adversity?

Is adversity experienced in the same way by everyone?

Does adversity affect people in different ways?

What does it mean to be strong?

If there is a God, how come terrible things keep happening in the world?

Is being strong always a good thing?

Does adversity always make you stronger?

Is weakness a bad thing?

Why do some people turn to God in times of adversity?

What is the point of prayer? (And does it do any good?)

Do people in other countries experience more or less adversity than people here? (And is it our problem anyway?)

Should we always help people who are experiencing adversity? (And what happens if we don't?)

Identifying a range of concepts that can be explored within a project doesn't mean we have to cover all of them, and it doesn't mean we can't be open to new ones that emerge as the project develops. If we come across different or new ways to thread aspects of the curriculum together, we should definitely embrace them – and if they come from the children, even better.

The process of designing enquiry questions, and in particular the identification of concepts, also helps us to decide which aspects of curriculum content we might adopt, which bits we might adapt and which bits we might ignore.

In terms of the curriculum, there will be some areas that appear to immediately link into a range of key concepts, and others that don't. There might also be some that fall into a kind of grey area – that are not obviously relevant but have potential. One example of this is an aspect of the geography curriculum to do with types of settlements. In lots of schools, this was covered via a range of seemingly random locations, from the exotic-sounding Chembakolli to the slightly less exotic-sounding Llandudno. It was all a bit insipid and none of it really mattered, so in terms of adopting, adapting or ignoring, it could come perilously close to being ditched. If, instead of throwing it out, we were to inter- pret the term 'settlements' more broadly, it's possible that it could then include work on the refugee crisis and, in particular, refugee camps or settlements. In terms of concepts, this could link directly to the themes of 'belonging', 'rights', 'freedom', 'cohesion' and 'integration', and suddenly this shift in focus transforms this area of the curriculum from meaningless to meaningful.

Having a rationale behind decisions like this is important – it means that we're not just using a scattergun approach to the parts of the curriculum we choose to explore in depth and the parts we choose to leave out. With careful thought, there will be lots of aspects that can be tied together into cohesive projects, but, equally, if an element of the curriculum doesn't provide an opportunity to explore the bigger ideas, then we're right to question why we're including it. After all, if we don't, the children will.

As we explored this process, one of the things that took me by surprise was just how passionately the teachers spoke about some of the content and concepts that started to emerge. In history, there were teachers who were desperate to cover particular time periods, partly because they loved them but also because they could see the potential for something more important than just subject content. Some of the areas aligned with the stuff we were supposed to be covering, and some didn't. Where it didn't match, we did it anyway. It was the same in the arts, geography and design technology. I was surprised because I'd never really witnessed it before. It can be hard to get excited about a curriculum that you just have to pick up and follow, but with the time to do things properly, and a shift in focus, it meant that all of a sudden there was the possibility of creating work worth caring about.

In a project developed for Year 5, the teachers settled on the Black Death as a focus for their history work. This might sound like a particularly gloomy period to go for, but we're quite close to the village of Eyam in Derbyshire, whose residents famously made the decision to quarantine themselves to prevent the plague spreading further. If you don't know the story it's well worth a quick look-up. In brief, the rector in the village, a man called William Mompesson, decided it was best to cut themselves off from the rest of the world, but then had to convince the other villagers. This was made more difficult by the fact that they didn't like him that much, and also by the knowledge that the self-imposed quarantine would mean almost certain death. Incredibly, they went for it and prepared themselves for the inevitable consequences. In total, 260 villagers died – roughly half the population of the village.

There's the potential here for an impressive topic name – in fact, after a quick search, I found a BBC news story titled: 'Eyam plague: The village of the damned'.[6] It's a tempting one, and I can even see the display I'd go for (all gothic and creepy, possibly graveyardy, with some fake spray-on spiderwebs thrown in for added impact), but, again, this is about me. Rather than focusing my creative thinking on how to present the learning, it's better applied to how I can tap into something bigger than just the historical events of the time.

If we look at the concept grid, there are several ideas that could be explored. One route to take would be to go for 'choice', 'free will' and 'common good'. The depth to which these concepts are developed will depend entirely on the responses of the children – it may be that there's one in particular that really captures their interest, or there might be several concepts that are explored over the course of the project. In *Dorothy Heathcote: Drama as a Learning Medium*, Betty Jane Wagner refers to a technique that Heathcote used when working with children

---

6 D. McKenna, Eyam Plague: The Village of the Damned, *BBC News* (5 November 2016). Available at: https://www.bbc.co.uk/news/uk-england-35064071.

called 'dropping to the universal'.[7] This is a useful way to introduce a concept to the children by making connections to existing shared understanding, truths or experiences. In this example, to begin the process of exploring 'choices', we can drop to the universal experiences that all the children have had, whether it's a choice of what they had for breakfast or a more significant decision, and from here we've got a starting point. The question designed to facilitate all of this was, 'Do our choices really matter?'

In terms of historical knowledge, the children will learn a lot about Eyam. This is important because through understanding the actions, behaviours and choices made in the past, we can start to question and explore exactly the same themes for ourselves in the present:

● How do choices make us feel?

● What is a dilemma?

● Is there a difference between a dilemma and a moral dilemma?

● What is free will?

● If I change my mind based on what someone else has said, is it still free will?

● How are our choices influenced by others? And does our behaviour influence the choices of others?

● Are there always consequences to our choices?

● What is the 'common good'?

● Should we always put others before ourselves?

● What is conscience?

Already, without getting too carried away, alongside the history we've now got RE, PSHE and philosophy emerging as important themes. When we add in the English work we could explore (e.g. narrative, diary, persuasive and discursive writing) and any other areas that would enhance the children's learning, then we're heading towards a pretty cohesive and meaningful structure for a project.

---

7   B. J. Wagner, *Dorothy Heathcote: Drama as a Learning Medium* (Portland, ME: Calendar Islands Publishers, 1999).

Exploring the kinds of concepts and questions sketched out above shouldn't just be the sole preserve of our oldest learners either. There's often the assumption that younger children can't have big thoughts because there's not that much in their heads. Anyone believing this should take themselves on a car journey with a five-year-old. Whilst being borderline painful, you'll be in no doubt about the size or importance of their ideas. One of my youngest daughter's classic questions was around what might happen if the road disappeared. The initial response of, 'Don't worry, it won't happen,' was quickly batted away with incessant follow-up questions until I found myself having to dredge up long-forgotten fragments of information about velocity, momentum and inertia, before finally arriving at the terrifying realisation that I might be stuck in the car with her as we continued our journey through infinite space. Young children have an incredible capacity for thinking, so the approach we adopt for exploring important concepts and themes should be used across the age range.

In Year 2, as part of a geography-themed project, the children were learning about the rainforest. This is a fairly common area to work on with young children but, again, in order to shift from simple curriculum coverage to something more, the concepts of 'responsibility', 'stewardship', 'consequences' and 'rights' were identified (other concepts are also available). This then led to the enquiry question, 'Do we always appreciate what we've got?'

As before, the approach opens up opportunity and possibility, and through the course of the project the children thought about the following questions:

- What does 'appreciate' mean?
- How do we show that we appreciate something? How do we give thanks?
- What are the things that we value the most?
- What are rights?
- What are privileges?
- What does it mean to 'take something for granted'?
- What if it's not there tomorrow?
- Do we always get what we deserve?
- If we don't own something, can it be ours?
- What is responsibility?

● Why should we care about things that might be happening on the other side of the world?

● Does the earth look after us or do we look after the earth?

The responses and additional questions that came from the children were amazing, and along with them becoming extremely knowledgeable about the physical geography of rainforests, there was also a tangible sense of their dissatisfaction with the lack of respect that humans seem to have for the planet. We didn't set out to teach empathy – I don't really think you can – but through the concepts explored and the thinking the children did, it took care of itself. They cared deeply about the rainforest, understood that it is everyone's responsibility to protect it and were angry about its destruction.

This response presents us with a different take on what constitutes a creative curriculum. Traditionally, I'd always associated creativity with children having fun. When I thought about creative teaching, it was linked to engagement and motivation – classrooms full of children having a brilliant time. Actually, it's not about making learning or the curriculum fun; it's about making it emotional. Quite often that emotion will be excitement, joy or inspiration, but to stop there would be to explore only part of what makes us human. What about dissatisfaction, anger or sadness?

If we're going to examine these feelings, we have to be careful. I wouldn't want the children to feel angry or sad if they weren't also enabled to do something about it. But, equally, we shouldn't shy away from addressing issues that may lead to these emotions just because we're dealing with young children.

One of our Year 1 projects began with the question, 'What does it mean to belong?' It was designed to allow the children to develop geographical knowledge about human features (e.g. cities, towns and houses). The theme of belonging also opened up the opportunity to explore the concepts of 'community', 'care', 'friendship', 'love' and 'social responsibility'. To get beyond the superficial sorting of different types of houses, the class teacher was interested in looking at the broader issue of homelessness. To help with this, she arranged for someone from the charity Shelter to come and speak to the children about homelessness at the start of the project. The visitor who came was amazing and spoke about her own personal experiences in a way that allowed the children to begin to understand some of the issues.

After chatting with the Year 1 pupils, it became apparent that they knew a lot more about homelessness than I might have imagined. For example, they told me that most homeless people don't actually live on the streets. They knew about 'inadequate housing' and 'rogue landlords' and the fact that having a home which wasn't in good condition was also classed as homelessness. As the project developed, the children added to their knowledge of geographical features whilst also continuing to explore issues around homelessness. Alongside this learning, they were also building a model of a home from an empty box. The design technology element of the project was intended to enable the children to think about the difference between a house and a home and then to use this to create their models. When the homes had been constructed, the teacher asked the children to bring in some small world figures from home so they could spend time playing with them.

The session began with all of the children playing happily with their figures in their beautifully decorated, furnished boxes. After letting this carry on for a while, the teacher then disappeared into her cupboard and emerged in role as a rogue landlord. The children fully understood this transition as she was always disappearing in there for one reason or another (a bit like Mr Benn, for those of you old enough to remember!). After walking around the classroom and ensuring that they were aware of her presence, she then approached a small group of children who were playing with their models and moved them away from the homes that they had lovingly created to some old tattered boxes that had been placed in the corner of the classroom. The group (who had been briefed before the start of the session) followed the instructions, moved to the tattered boxes and continued to play. The response from the other children was, at first, to simply carry on playing as before – they were unaffected and so didn't seem to notice.

Gradually, the teacher evicted more and more children and sent them to play with the damaged boxes until one little girl called her over. When the teacher/rogue landlord asked her what she wanted, she asked why her friend had been told to leave her home to go and play with the 'messy' boxes. The teacher explained that it was because they couldn't have the nice house any more – she had decided they had to leave. The girl thought for a few seconds, and then said, 'But that's not fair.'

At this point, the teacher stopped everything, came out of role, and gathered the children together in a circle. She asked the little girl to repeat what she'd just said for the others to hear, and then started to explore what it meant. Throughout the discussion, the children spoke about why they thought that nobody had noticed to begin with and whether the evicted people would feel any sense of belonging. In answering their enquiry question, 'What does it mean to belong?' the children were able to recognise that there are frequently people who don't feel like they belong, and that part of this can come from being ignored or feeling invisible. The children were angry that there are individuals who have to live in situations where they don't have a sense of belonging or even have their basic needs met.

To leave the project at this point would have been wrong – the children needed to know that it's OK to feel angry, but also that we can use this emotion to do something positive to make a difference. In terms of the concepts, there isn't any point in understanding 'social responsibility' or 'justice' unless it leads to action, and in this case, the sense of empowerment came from the children highlighting the work of the charity Shelter (through showcasing the work they'd done in class) and also by fundraising to support the charity's projects.

The action taken in this example is visible and obvious, but this doesn't always need to be the case. Even something as simple as a shift in understanding or a commitment to thinking differently can have a significant impact on children's lives.

The geography example on settlements that we touched on earlier led to a Year 5 project that began with the question, 'What is the difference between surviving and living?' Along with the concepts of 'belonging', 'rights' and 'cohesion', the teachers also picked out themes around 'media' and 'protest' as part of learning about the European refugee crisis. The project began with the children discussing the questions and concepts and offering their initial thoughts about the kind of things that we need to survive. This then developed over the course of the project into an exploration of human rights and the further question of whether it's ever OK to restrict or remove people's rights. The children researched the experience of refugees, including those living in long-established camps like Kakuma in Kenya as well as in short-term settlements like the 'Jungle' in Calais.

Exploring the movement of people led them to issues around migration and the portrayal of migrants in the media. Towards the end of the project, the children were presented with a range of newspaper headlines from the British press. One reference to migrants as a 'swarm' caused horror and outrage, and began a discussion about how and why a word usually applied to insects could be used to label groups of people who were desperately trying to improve their life chances.[8] The children wanted to do something, and by making a commitment to challenge lazy stereotypes, think critically about messages portrayed in the media and ignore the labels used to demean others, they took possibly the most important action they could.

Exploring issues like this with children can be contentious, and I've had some interesting conversations with teachers who don't agree that it's appropriate. My argument centres on the fact that what we're doing is giving the children the opportunity to think, rather than telling them what to think. We showed the children a range of different headlines on the migrant crisis from as many different newspapers as possible – to simply select the front pages that served a particular purpose, political or otherwise, would have been irresponsible. The fact that the children focused on the sensationalist language used in one particular publication was a result of the empathy they had developed over the course of the project. If, as a result of this, they came to view certain publications or people in a different light, then this was their thought process and decision, not ours.

We used the same approach with all of the concepts explored through the projects. Our aim was to build the children's knowledge and skill, make space for thinking and then allow them to use that space to think for themselves and make up their own minds.

---

8   C. Ellicott and S. Wright, The 'Swarm' on Our Streets, *Daily Mail* (31 July 2015).

Chapter 6

'LOVE AND HUGS, DAVE C.'

With an enquiry question as a starting point, and ideas about the concepts and issues that could be explored, we're now ready to think about another key aspect of projects – the connection to authentic outcomes and critical audiences.

We can't expect children to produce incredible work if it's only ever going to be stuck in a book. I've never had a child ask me outright why I was making them do a particular task, but I'm pretty sure there have been times when they have been thinking it. Having a purpose is a key motivating factor with a project; whatever they're doing has to matter.

In the past I've lied to children about the reasons for doing things. I once forged a letter from the then Prime Minister David Cameron for a class of Year 6 pupils. I told the children that he had decided to change the denomination of coins that were being produced by the Royal Mint. All coins, with the exception of the 5p, were to be removed from circulation and a brand new 3p was to be minted. They were not best pleased, but when their anger subsided they decided (with some encouragement from me) that they should try to find out whether or not they could pay for any given item with only the two coins at their disposal.

Whilst taking a moment to congratulate myself on having conned them into some maths work, I also decided that I could squeeze some persuasive writing out of them by getting them to write back to the PM to present their findings. We spent a lovely two weeks working on our persuasive devices and putting together an appropriately compelling response. When the writing unit finished, I was ready to move on to something else that I'd sneakily made up. Except the children didn't want to move on. They wanted to post the letters. I hadn't counted on this. The letters were written in their books ready for me to mark but, as one young man pointed out, you can't post an English book to the leader of the country.

From the outset, I hadn't tried to make the lie massively believable – I'd written the original letter from the PM in wobbly blue crayon. It was even signed 'Love and hugs, Dave C.'. This obviously hadn't registered, and now we were in the position of them believing the whole thing. As I saw it, I had two options: either come clean and tell them I made it up or let them actually send the letters. I decided to take my chances with Mr Cameron and let him face the barrage of abuse about an imaginary policy of which he had absolutely no knowledge. I know it wasn't the right choice, but I thought it was better in the long term that they felt let down by him rather than by me.

The intrinsic motivation gained from believing something to be real is incredibly powerful. To avoid lying to the children, one option would be to present the scenario as fictional from the start. In my experience, children will happily buy into a story in the knowledge that they'll have a much better time if they go along with it than if they don't. The second, and perhaps most obvious option, is to actually do something real in the first place. For this, the children need to be working towards an authentic outcome that will sustain their interest and enthusiasm throughout the project. If we're looking to go beyond the children completing work just to fill a book or, worse still, to satisfy some misguided call for 'evidence', then how they showcase their learning, and who they showcase it to, becomes massively important.

By using broad enquiry questions, there will always be a number of avenues that can be explored in terms of an outcome. It may be that one particular strand of the project becomes the focus for an outcome or it may be that it's the whole lot. This can depend on the opportunities we've managed to identify and also on the direction that the children are interested in taking.

One of the most straightforward ways to create an outcome is to work towards an exhibition. Exhibiting children's work is nothing new – we've always celebrated work by adding it to displays in classrooms or around the building. If we're interested in upping the ante, however, we can look beyond the school to public spaces.

In *An Ethic of Excellence*, Ron Berger questions the usefulness of parents as an audience for children's work.[1] Obviously, it's a good thing for work to be shared with parents, but his point is that parents typically like everything their children produce. This will ring true for anyone who has children of their own. They will bring all sorts home from school – a pile of misshapen cardboard boxes wrapped in sticky tape that is apparently a Roman fort, random bits of coloured card glued onto a sheet of paper (with glitter) or crumbling fragments of air-dried

---

1   R. Berger, *An Ethic of Excellence: Building a Culture of Craftsmanship with Students* (Portsmouth, NH: Heinemann, 2003).

clay that once looked a little bit like a caterpillar. You can see them watching you closely for your reaction, and you would have to be pretty hard-hearted to respond with anything other than complete positivity. You then have to proudly display whatever it is, before picking just the right moment a few weeks later to transfer it into the garage/bin without anyone noticing.

It's the same with performances. As a teacher, I've watched some horrific nativity plays that have been greeted with standing ovations from parents. We can't help ourselves, and we should be delighted with the things our children show us. But from a school perspective, it leaves us with a problem. If children get the message that whatever they produce will be greeted with praise, then they will settle for this as the expected standard.

What we really need, if we're going to get the children to produce brilliant work, is a less forgiving audience, and, fortunately, we don't have to look that far to find one. Taking advantage of the unsuspecting general public is a great way to ensure a critical audience, and the knowledge that their work is going to be exhibited 'out there' in the real world has an incredible effect on the children. All of a sudden there's pressure. Applying pressure to children is not normally seen as a good thing, but in this case, it's a positive incentive. When they realise their work is going to be viewed by people other than their teacher and parents, then it's got to be better.

There are lots of places in which to exhibit children's work – from the dramatic backdrop of a National Trust property or a museum, to the less flashy walls of a dentist's waiting room. Where it happens isn't as important as the fact that it's out there.

Along with location, another way of creating a worthwhile outcome is to think about how the work will be exhibited. During one of our early projects that began with the question, 'Does the camera ever lie?' the children built up their knowledge of light and shadow, then developed their photography skills to create images that captured a range of different optical illusions. Along with the knowledge that their work would be exhibited in a public space, another key motivator was the fact that the photographs would be framed. For lots of the children, this was the thing they were most excited about – their work, if it was good enough, would be put into a frame and hung on a wall. When the public exhibition finished, the framed prints were displayed in a corridor in the school and you could hear the children proudly pointing out which photograph was theirs as they walked past.

If we take this further, what difference would it make if, rather than displaying the children's work on a windowsill or table, it was presented in a glass cabinet? Thanks to the Swedish flat-pack furniture specialists, the cost of this isn't great, but the value added to the children's projects is huge.

What we're doing here is giving a very clear message that we view the children as professionals or, at the very least, as people capable of producing professional work. To get an idea about what that professional work should or could look like, it might be that rather than just making use of the general public, we could aim instead for specific individuals with particular areas of expertise.

I first got chatting to Barbara thanks to a random internet search whilst looking for ideas about authentic outcomes for some of our history projects. Barbara is seventy-eight years old (it was one of the first things she told me) and the chairperson of a local history group. We hit it off straight away, and after chatting for a couple of minutes, it became apparent that this could well have been the first official phone call that the group had ever received. After I explained the work we were doing in school, she told me that she would be delighted to help us in any way she could. Would we be able to bring the children to a meeting so they could present their work to the group? Absolutely! Would the group be interested in coming into school to provide a critical audience for our children? They'd love to!

No matter what I asked, Barbara came back with a positive response, and before long, I'd been made an honorary member of the history group and was booked in for their Christmas do. The fact that I got such a positive response encouraged me to make more phone calls, and it turned out that there were experts and professionals all over the place who were desperate to be involved in our projects.

Because of the pressure schools have been under for as long as I can remember, lots of us have become quite insular and stopped looking outwards. I suppose it's a survival strategy but, actually, beyond the benefits in terms of motivation and raised expectations, there's another really important reason why we should make an effort to build these connections back up again.

One of the side effects of having a packed curriculum is that any additional stuff you might want to do tends to get squeezed into themed days or weeks. In the worst cases, it could be that some monumentally important aspect of being human, like creativity, gets done via a whole-school Creative Week sometime in June. In other cases, it could be a World Book Day, Refugee Week, Healthy Eating Fortnight or Black History Month. I'm not a fan of any of this, but not because I don't think they're important issues. It's more because confining them to just a day or a week doesn't make them important enough. These are all things that should be woven into projects instead of being crammed in as an afterthought.

Careers education is another area that fits into this bracket as it's something which has the potential to have a huge impact on children's lives, particularly the pupils at my school. I was given careers advice when I was at sixth-form college in the early 1990s. I think there might have been a man in an office whose job it was to do the advising, but I'm not sure I came into contact with him. Instead, I received my guidance from one of the computers that sat in the library. This computer was incredible. Before writing this, I had a quick look on the internet for some more up-to-date career quizzes and there are plenty out there. If you complete one of these you get a write-up at the end about the kinds of jobs that might suit your personality, but it's all a bit vague and unfulfilling. The software that we had was much more decisive. It didn't mess about with a range of careers – it churned out one. No grey areas, this is the job for you; get on with it.

I didn't have a clue about what job I wanted to do. I'm not one of those people who always wanted to be a teacher. I wanted a proper job – something easy that paid lots of money. I was excited about the careers guidance software. It didn't matter that I didn't know what to do with my life because the computer would. The fifty or so questions were all multiple-choice and I answered them as truthfully as I could. It took forever, but I finally got to the 'click for results' bit. What happened next turned out to be a massive let-down. It transpired that my ideal career was the relatively niche position of 'French polisher'.

Now, I've got nothing against furniture polishers, French or otherwise, but it wasn't the advice I was hoping for, and, if I'm totally honest, I'm not convinced that careers education has moved on that much in the past twenty years. Ex-pupils I've spoken to over the last few years report the mixed quality of advice they've been given. In most cases it's patchy – a visiting speaker at some point in Year 10 or a hastily cobbled together work experience week somewhere they didn't want to go in the first place.

For some children it doesn't actually matter. Some children have their paths mapped out for them, and whilst the detail of what this might look like will evolve over time, their route to 'success' is pretty much sorted. For these children, expectation and aspiration is the norm; throw into the mix a 'careers day', when the doctors, architects and solicitors get rolled out, and it's job done.

For other children it really matters. My school sits in an area of high deprivation. Expectation and aspiration are not always the norm, and the cycle that children and families find themselves in can be incredibly difficult to break. Careers days, or even weeks, are at best a waste of time, and at worst a well-intentioned but ultimately patronising glimpse of a life that the young people feel is completely out of reach.

A large number of the children I've worked with over the last twenty years have fragile self-esteem and low levels of self-belief and self-confidence. Changing their thinking takes time and can never be 'fixed' with one-off interventions, motivational posters or focus weeks that are bolted onto the curriculum. To shift children's thinking, aspiration and opportunity need to be constantly drip-fed from the moment they enter our schools until the moment they leave.

If the children are attempting to curate an exhibition, then it makes perfect sense to bring in a curator and pick their brains. If that professional is also able to revisit when the children have completed their project, then we have a ready-made critical audience – someone who can accurately appraise their work because that's exactly what they do for a living.

There's the potential in any project to build in this kind of careers link, and if we're using this model all the way through school, then that's a huge number of people the children get to learn alongside. By the time our children reach Year 6, they've worked with metallurgists, engineers, conservationists, landscape designers, river and water management specialists, sustainability planners, sculptors, ceramicists, historians, curators, authors, illustrators, poets, emergency management specialists, caregivers, religious leaders, costume designers, filmmakers, musicians, dancers – and this list keeps growing year on year.

Alongside the obvious benefits this brings in terms of making the children aware of a range of occupations and professions, working with professionals also has a huge impact on their language. There seems to be some debate at the moment over the best way to build children's vocabulary (in particular that of disadvantaged groups). Everyone agrees that language is one of the key elements we should be working on – that isn't the issue. As usual, the problems begin when we start thinking about how.

There's no question that one of the best ways to develop a rich vocabulary with children is to read to them as much as possible and, beyond this, to encourage them to read a wide range of high quality texts for themselves. The explicit teaching of language is also important, particularly through the writing process, but there's another key element of language development that doesn't seem to get the credit it deserves.

Experiences, particularly the conversations that children have with adults, are just as much a part of developing language as the factors mentioned previously. Projects involving trips to castles, museums, zoos or theatres all have a massive impact on the amount of language to which children are exposed. When you add in the professionals who not only lend authenticity to the projects but also bring with them specialist terminology, then we've got a model that encourages the development and use of language – not just for the sake of it, but because it matters to the success of our project.

Over the past couple of years, our children have built an incredible range of vocabulary thanks entirely to the projects and the experts working alongside them: Year 3 children discussing the relative merits of their maquettes; Year 4 children agonising over the depth of their marginal planting and worrying about invasive pond species; Year 2 children who know that pig iron isn't something you find on a farm.

A well-designed project should be bursting with language, and rather than leaving it to chance, the vocabulary that the children will encounter can be identified whilst the project is being planned. For example, the Year 4 pond-building project gave the children an opportunity not just to learn but also to use the following vocabulary about ecosystems:

- **Algae**: A simple non-flowering aquatic plant.
- **Amphibian**: A cold-blooded vertebrate.
- **Aquatic (plant)**: Growing in or near water.
- **Colonise**: When a plant or animal establishes itself in an area.
- **Consumer**: An organism that feeds on other organisms.

- **Ecosystem**: A community of living things that interact with each other and their environment.

- **Emergent (plant)**: An aquatic plant with leaves and flowers that appear above the water's surface.

- **Environment**: The conditions in which a person, animal or plant lives or operates.

- **Habitat**: The natural home or environment of an animal, plant or other organism (living thing).

- **Invasive species**: A non-native species that changes or disrupts an ecosystem.

- **Invertebrate**: An animal that does not have a backbone (spine).

- **Marginal (plant)**: Plants that grow around the edges of water.

- **Microorganism**: A microscopic organism.

- **Native**: An animal or plant that belongs to a particular place.

- **Non-native**: An animal or plant that does not belong to a particular place.

- **Nutrient**: Something that provides nourishment (food) for life and growth.

- **Organic**: Connected with, produced by or coming from living things.

- **Organism**: An individual animal, plant or single-celled life form.

- **Oxygenating plant (submerged aquatic)**: Fast-growing plants that give out oxygen.

- **Producer**: An organism that makes its own nutrients (food).

- **Reptile**: A type of vertebrate that includes lizards, snakes, crocodiles, turtles and tortoises.

- **Species**: A group of organisms made up of similar individuals.

- **Vegetation**: Plants that are found in a particular area or habitat.

- **Vertebrate**: An animal with a backbone (spine).

This kind of immersive and proactive approach to building language seems to be a better way of working than the deficit model. I'm not interested in starting with a Key Stage 2 SATs reading paper and working backwards, and I've got even less interest in second guessing what might crop up in future tests.

Developing the range of opportunities available to our children and surrounding them with people who have made a career out of their interests, talents and passions means that they get to develop a formidable range of language whilst at the same time experiencing what's out there for themselves.

After all, if you've already curated an exhibition aged seven-and-a-half, then what's to stop you making a career of it?

Chapter 7
SOFTLY, SOFTLY, CATCHEE MONKEY

With the kind of intrinsically motivating projects that we're building here, there's a very good chance that the children won't want to produce anything other than their very best work. To make absolutely sure of this, though, there's one more layer that we can add to support our drive for incredibleness.

We've already looked at how authentic outcomes and critical audiences can impact on the children's desire to produce professional-looking work, but there should also be the recognition that very little of any value is ever created with ease or, at the very least, at the first time of asking.

I've already mentioned Ron Berger and his brilliant book *An Ethic of Excellence*. Along with his suggestion that we look for the kind of critical audiences that won't tolerate rubbish, he is also interested in creating a culture in which children don't settle for their first attempt at a piece of work, or even their second or third.

The process of producing multiple drafts is not a new thing and most of us have been up to something like this when planning writing units. In fact, you can't actually deliver the English curriculum without building in time for editing and redrafting. What hadn't particularly occurred to me was that this might be an approach that we could use across the whole curriculum. Thanks to the legacy of trying to cover everything, in almost every subject other than writing we'd only ever go for a second draft if the children had messed up their first attempt to the extent that it was completely unrecoverable. With our 'less is more' approach there wasn't the same excuse, and with more time, we reckoned we could use the idea of creating multiple drafts more widely.

In terms of this even being an option, everything we've looked at in terms of the concept-based learning approach and building authentic outcomes is essential. If we're considering moving towards multiple drafts, then the children have got to care about what they're doing. If they're not bothered about their work (or don't see the purpose), then making them redraft it is painful for everyone involved. They won't want to do it and will resent you forcing them into it. On the other hand, if they are immersed in their project and are desperate to produce something amazing, then they will be willing to produce draft after draft to make sure their work is as good as it can possibly be.

For this to work effectively, there needs to be clear guidance throughout the whole process. There's no point creating a first draft if you have no idea where to start, and it's just as pointless producing more drafts unless you've had some very specific feedback on how to improve. Rather than this coming solely from the teacher, the use of rubrics (a posh word for success criteria) and critique promotes high levels of independence from the children. Work always starts with an exemplar (sometimes called a WAGOLL – What A Good One Looks Like), which is then used to generate warm and cool feedback (which we will come to shortly). Berger's mantra for making sure that the feedback is good enough is that it must be 'kind', 'specific' and 'helpful'.[1]

To make sure that the process of generating feedback was properly embedded we spent a long time practising it. This sounds like common sense, but thanks to the ridiculousness of the school improvement culture, quite often, if you're not implementing something and demonstrating its impact within a matter of weeks, you're written off as a failure. For reasonable people like us, it's obvious that this is complete rubbish – to do anything properly takes time, and for us, this meant devoting an entire term just to getting the language right.

To get off on the right foot, seeds need to be planted with even the very youngest children in the school. For nursery or Foundation Stage 1, there isn't any formal use of the critique process because it isn't appropriate. What is important, though, is to begin the groundwork that will make life easier for the children as they get older. This really boils down to one little phrase that carries an incredibly important message. We're usually delighted with anything our four-year-olds do. This is fine, but there's a chance that our loveliness and positivity about the picture they've made from three dried pasta shells and two litres of PVA glue might be giving them the wrong message. It's important that we're still positive with them, but instead of saying, 'What an amazing picture!' a shift to 'That's an amazing picture – what a great start!' could begin to embed a subconscious understanding that there are always improvements to be made. At this stage, 'What a great start' is nothing more than a phrase, and I wouldn't for a second make a four-year-old redraft their pasta picture – for starters, they've probably

---

1   See https://www.youtube.com/watch?v=cWMH_X4IvOk.

used up all the glue. What we're after here is the slow drip-feeding of an attitude – the beginnings of a culture that can then be developed.

To continue this process into reception (Foundation Stage 2) and up through the rest of the school, we began by building the children's use of warm feedback language. In my experience, children are pretty good at providing critical feedback, and while this is useful, we didn't necessarily want it to be their default setting. To start with, we used stock phrases that we wanted the children to replicate. These sentence starters were displayed in every classroom (always on pink card) and we took every opportunity we could to use them.

'I really liked the way ...'

'What jumped out was ...'

'My favourite part is ...'

'My eye was drawn to ...'

These might seem a bit contrived, but that's because they are. I'm not usually a fan of this level of prescriptiveness, but in this case, we wanted the children to see the critique process as something new and important, rather than as an opportunity to have a chat about the bits they liked.

In terms of practising, there were plenty of opportunities across the curriculum. The list below is not meant to be exhaustive but it is a start.

Art: A sketch, drawing, illustration, painting or sculpture.

Design technology: A diagram, blueprint or finished product.

English: An extract from a novel, book or particular genre of writing.

Geography: A map, plan, model, diagram or report.

History: A replica document, an artefact or an explanation text.

Maths: A calculation, solution, table, graph or chart.

PE: A film clip of a professional gymnast or athlete.

RE: A piece of scripture (e.g. psalm), an illuminated manuscript or an illustration.

Science: A diagram, report or table of results.

The exemplar pieces of work were either created or found by us, which meant that we were able to make sure our expectations were high enough. Of the three key elements to successful feedback, being kind was mostly sorted because of the innate niceness of the children. The other two took quite a lot of work to get right. Beyond the difficulties of just pronouncing the word 'specific', the children also found it hard to generate feedback that did the job that was needed.[2] To get around this, we treated the process as if it were any other area of the curriculum that was proving tricky and modelled it for them.

English: Extract from a novel

'I disappeared on the night before my twelfth birthday. July 28, 1988. Only now can I at last tell the whole extraordinary story, the true story. Kensuke made me promise that I would say nothing, nothing at all, until at least ten years had passed. It was almost the last thing he said to me. I promised, and because of that I have had to live out a lie.'

Michael Morpurgo – *Kensuke's Kingdom*[3]

Focus: Identify sentences that create mystery or intrigue.

Exemplar critique – warm feedback:

'I really like the way that he uses the word "extraordinary" to let us know straight away that what we're going to read will be amazing.'

'My eye was drawn to the opening sentence. It's a simple sentence and it grabs the reader's attention – someone disappearing is dramatic – I want to know what happened!'

'What jumped out was the way that he uses more than one way of adding mystery – I want to know how he disappeared, who Kensuke was, why he had to make a promise and why he had to wait ten years.'

---

2 It's not just the children who find this difficult – how many of the comments used in written marking by teachers are specific enough to be useful? And even if they are, do the children understand it sufficiently and have the time to do anything productive with it? I don't want to get into marking and feedback, but it's definitely an area we need to be thinking about. How much of what we've traditionally done has any impact on learning?

3 M. Morpurgo, *Kensuke's Kingdom* (London: Egmont, 2017 [1999]), p. 1.

Maths: Calculation

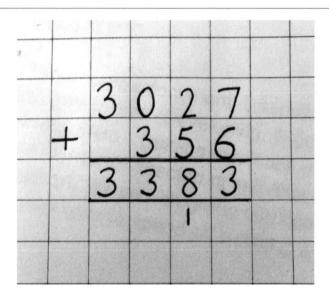

Focus: Column addition.

Exemplar critique – warm feedback:

'My eye was drawn to the way the digits are lined up carefully in the correct columns.'

'I really like the way that the "ten" is recorded clearly underneath the line.'

'What jumped out was how neatly the calculation is recorded … each digit is in its own square.'

Geography: Diagram

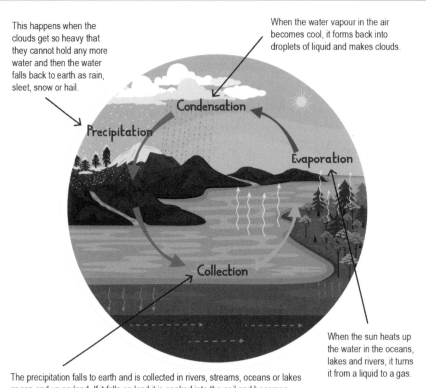

This happens when the clouds get so heavy that they cannot hold any more water and then the water falls back to earth as rain, sleet, snow or hail.

When the water vapour in the air becomes cool, it forms back into droplets of liquid and makes clouds.

Condensation

Precipitation

Evaporation

Collection

When the sun heats up the water in the oceans, lakes and rivers, it turns it from a liquid to a gas.

The precipitation falls to earth and is collected in rivers, streams, oceans or lakes or can end up on land. If it falls on land it is soaked into the soil and becomes groundwater. The precipitation will also run over the soil and into streams, rivers, lakes and, eventually, the ocean, where the whole cycle will start again.

Focus: Understand and describe the water cycle.

Exemplar critique – warm feedback:

'My eye was drawn to the way the arrows help you to move around the cycle.'

'I really like the way that each key word is explained with a short section of text.'

'My favourite part is the drawing. It lets you see every part of the cycle and helps you to make sense of the explanations.'

Science: Table of results

Object	Height of bounce (cm)		
Tennis ball	25.5cm	23.0cm	24.5cm
Golf ball	38.0cm	35.5cm	36.5cm
Sponge ball	12.5cm	14.0cm	13.0cm
Cricket ball	15.0cm	16.5cm	16.5cm

Context: The children are investigating how what material a ball is made from affects the height of its bounce.

Focus: Recording results in a table.

Exemplar critique – warm feedback:

'I really like the way they have repeated the experiment to get three sets of results for each ball. This will make it more reliable.'

'What jumped out was how they had measured accurately to the nearest half centimetre.'

'My eye was drawn to the way that the table is set out. The columns and rows are labelled so it's clear and easy to understand.'

Over time (remember this was the focus for a whole term), the children started using the warm feedback phrases without any prompting and got better and better at providing statements that were actually of some use. In Key Stage 2, the vast majority of the children wrote their own feedback on some pink sticky notes we'd bought in specially. In Key Stage 1, there was more of a mix, with the teachers sometimes scribing the feedback for the children (as a whole class) and at other times letting them have a go for themselves.

With the basics in place, we then taught the children how to turn their warm feedback into statements for a rubric. Given how confident they all were this was fairly easy, and within the space of a few weeks they got the idea of taking their feedback, sticking a verb at the front of it and adding it to their rubric.

Warm feedback	Rubric statement
'My eye was drawn to the opening sentence. It's a simple sentence and it grabs the reader's attention.'	Use a simple sentence to grab the reader's attention.
'I really like the way that the "ten" is recorded clearly underneath the line.'	Record the 'ten' clearly underneath the line.
'What jumped out was how they had measured accurately to the nearest half centimetre.'	Measure accurately to the nearest half centimetre.

When the children were happily writing their own rubric statements based on warm feedback, we then introduced them to the language we wanted them to use for cool feedback (this time on blue card) and repeated the whole process again:

'Could you …?'

'Why don't you try …?'

'A good idea would be …'

'Have you considered …?'

'Have you thought of …?'

Even though we were deliberately taking things slowly, this part was quite quick because the children understood what was going on – they were simply extending what they had done before, and the same rules around being kind, specific and helpful still applied. At this point (about two terms in), the children were independently writing their own rubrics based on feedback they had generated for themselves. When we'd started the process, we were most interested in the end point – getting to the stage where the children could provide peer critique to each other. What we'd overlooked was the impact of the steps in-between: the independence involved in creating rubrics for themselves had made a massive and unexpected difference to the children. It turned out that they actually used the rubrics when they were producing their own work.

We'd always used things like success criteria, but these had always been written by the teacher and given to or shared with the children. Although this has long been considered good practice, I'd always had a sneaking suspicion that the children only ever pretended to use them. This will be a familiar scenario to most teachers who have experienced using some form of success criteria with children. The checklists spell out what the children need to include in their writing: we share it with them, teach it to them and print out a copy so they've got it next to them before they start their 'big write' or whatever else we call it. From a quick survey of the class at the end of the writing session, we start to get pretty excited about the quality of their work as it appears they've all ticked off everything on the list. We then take the work home to mark and discover that they've lied to us. They might have ticked off the items, but it bears absolutely no relation to what they've actually written.

I don't know exactly why producing the rubrics for themselves made such a difference, but it's probably to do with the fact that because they created them, there was ownership, and as a result, they actually cared enough (and also remembered) to use them. The form this process took was dictated by the age group we were working with. Whilst the older children were capable of writing the rubrics for themselves, in Key Stage 1 and the Early Years Foundation Stage (EYFS) the children often worked as a whole class, jointly suggesting ideas which the teacher then wrote up as they went along.

By this stage (about term three-ish), everything we needed to get to the peer critique was in place. To ease us into this, we used a technique called 'gallery critique', which basically involved displaying the children's work around the classroom and allowing them to move around and leave feedback on each other's work. This is a good way to start; because it's anonymous, the children found it non-threatening and they loved going back to their work to find the feedback that had been left. In the excitement that came from being allowed to move around the room, sometimes the quality of feedback tended to slip, but just as before, we used this as an opportunity to model the specificity we wanted.

The peer critique part was the last layer. We kept up with the gallery critique because this whole-class approach is a brilliant way to check the quality of feedback being given, but when you've got to this stage, there's no reason why the children can't select their own critique partners and go through the process for themselves.

Exploring this approach over the course of the year threw up some interesting thoughts around the sequencing of learning and the importance of using critique at the right time. For example, for the feedback to be specific and helpful, it needs subject-specific knowledge or skills to back it up. In one piece of work, a group of Year 5 children were creating pencil drawings of a zebra's head. Given that stripes feature quite heavily in any representation of a zebra, it wasn't surprising that it was something they spotted in the exemplar piece that was shown to them. And the reason we know they spotted them was because they said so quite explicitly in their warm feedback:

'I really like the stripes.'

Now, as an observation, you can't fault it, but as a helpful piece of feedback that could be turned into a rubric statement, the best you could end up with would be 'draw stripes'. This is where having specific knowledge and skills – in this case in art – really makes a difference. If the children had already learnt about the principle of contrast, then they could have used this to create much more specific and therefore helpful feedback:

'I really like the way the spacing between the stripes creates contrast.'

And from this, they've got the chance to generate a statement for their own rubric that will actually make a difference to their work:

'Use spacing between the stripes to create contrast.'

Recognising the link between specificity and knowing or being able to do stuff can also help us to identify which bits of the curriculum we can easily have a go at and which bits might be left until later.

Writing is a good example of something that we were initially tempted to use critique with until it dawned on us that this is actually a pretty complicated area. For it to be of any use, the children would need enough grammatical knowledge to ensure that any feedback given was specific and helpful. If their knowledge and understanding of grammar were sketchy, then they would just end up making nice comments about the quality of the presentation or handwriting rather than anything that would actually improve the quality of the writing.

A quick and easy way of ensuring that the children use their prior learning (and a good way of double checking that they actually know what they're talking about) is to encourage them to add an 'e.g.' to their feedback.

If we take writing as an example, a child could give the following feedback:

'My eye was drawn to the adjectives that were used.'

As a piece of feedback, it's not doing a particularly great job in terms of specificity, and it's also possible that the child has written it because at some point they've heard that adjectives are a good thing to put into writing; whether or not they actually know what an adjective is, though, is anyone's guess.

With an 'e.g.', you demonstrate that you actually know what you're talking about:

'My eye was drawn to the adjectives that were used, *e.g. "sinister" and "menacing"*.'

This could be classed as adding the 'what' – the e.g. tells us that they remember what an adjective is. To develop the feedback further we could also add a 'why':

'My eye was drawn to the adjectives that were used *to describe the main character*, e.g. "sinister" and "menacing".'

What we've got here is something that would definitely make a difference. The pupil has picked the adjectives out of an exemplar or another child's work, they clearly understand what they're talking about (because they already know it or they've just learnt about it) and they know why they're useful words to include.

In terms of redrafting, whether it's in English, art, science, geography or whatever else we decide to apply this to, we've now got a structure that gives us a clear idea about what we're aiming for, as well as a means of getting there. The more work that goes into helping the children to fine-tune their critique, the better and more useful their rubrics will be, and the greater chance there is of them producing multiple drafts of increasing quality.

This process fits perfectly with the idea of the children working on authentic outcomes, and also does away with the often frantic way in which we deal with children's work in school. When I first started teaching, displays needed to be changed at least every half-term. This was hard work, especially if you had a lot of boards to fill, so because of the inevitable rush, I don't think I thought too hard about what was going up, as long as it was double-mounted and not too wonky.

If the children care about their work, and they've been through the process of redrafting, they will produce stuff that deserves to be displayed or exhibited for longer than six weeks. We've got some work in school that's been up for years because it's incredible, and most work will be displayed for at least a year. With the photography project I mentioned earlier, the work was exhibited in a public gallery for two weeks. After this, it came back to school and was displayed in the corridor for another twelve months. Along with the pride this generated in the children, it also meant we had a ready-made starting point for similar projects in the future. If a different class or the following year's cohort were looking for exemplars of high quality photography to begin the process of critique, then we had them. When the children create brilliant work, we keep hold of it because it feeds directly into the production of more brilliant work, and year on year, the quality is pushed higher and higher as the children's expectations are edged upwards.

It might seem that the year we spent embedding all of this was a little excessive, but I think approaching it cautiously and building bit by bit is probably one of the best decisions we made. As a direct result of adding critique to our concept-based learning approach, we've got children who have developed an almost obsessive attention to detail and the ability to speak articulately about the learning process. The sense of pride that comes from producing incredible work is addictive, and before they know it, they're trapped in a cycle of brilliance that's impossible to escape.

Chapter 8

HITCHES AND HICCUPS

To recap, we've considered the skills that could form the basis of our projects, the content and concepts that could be explored, the enquiry questions that we can use as starting points, the layers of authenticity that can be added to produce incredible work and, finally, the process of critique that will help to get us there.

Before examining what all this looks like in the classroom, there are a couple of other areas that are worth considering, which can help us to overcome some of the problems that can crop up when working on projects.

One of the first issues that we had to iron out was the tendency to slip back into a subject-focused approach rather than to view the project as a whole. Traditionally, we had always been very keen on labelling specific lessons or pieces of learning – it comes from our obsession with timetables. Most schools love a good timetable, and one of our jobs as teachers has been to fill it with the subjects we'll be teaching. The mornings were pretty straightforward – five lots of English and five lots of maths. We'd then squeeze everything else into the afternoons, with boxes for science, PE, history, art or whatever else we were doing at the time. I'll talk about how we might look at this differently later on, but for now, this way of organising the timetable presents us with a problem when designing a cohesive project.

The minute we start falling back into subject boxes, we lose the sense of working on something bigger. I say this because working within the boundaries of subjects on a timetable isn't a natural state for children, and it definitely isn't how they began their experience of education. I've talked to a lot of four- and five-year-old children about their learning, and not once in all of the conversations I've had have they responded by telling me that they're developing their 'understanding of the world', or fine-tuning their 'communication and language' or brushing up on their 'understanding of expressive arts and design'. They're just learning, and they have absolutely no interest in where the edges are or what particular area of learning they happen to be focusing on in any given moment.

In the Early Years, teachers hold on to the knowledge of which areas are being worked on, but they don't feel the urge to label it or share it with the children.

This doesn't appear to impede them in any way because, ultimately, learning is learning. This thinking needs to filter through to the way in which the rest of us manage our projects. We might have a timetable and it might have subject areas written on it, but the best thing we can do is to hide it away and start to blur the lines. The attitude we need to foster in the classroom is one that constantly draws the children (and us) back to the concepts we're exploring. This is what will bring everything together – we're not doing English, history, RE or PSHE, we're working on our project.

For this to work, it has to become a mantra – something you say to yourself as much as to the children. There will be nothing blurry about the learning – we know exactly what the children will be learning about and so will they. Labelling it with a specific subject title is unnecessary. To begin with, the children might question you about this: 'Was that RE we were doing or English?' But after a while, if you've really cracked it, they will stop asking the question altogether and just become absorbed in their work.

One quick and easy way to remind ourselves that the project question and concepts are the most important thing is to make sure that they're displayed as prominently as possible in the classroom. Have them spanning an entire wall or peg big sheets of card to a washing line and string it across the classroom – whatever you do, and however creatively you do it, it needs to be unmissable. The question display can also become a focal point for emerging thoughts, ideas and questions that crop up as the project progresses, regardless of which subject area they've come from. Again, this is a good way to emphasise that everything we're doing is feeding into our project and the desire to answer our question.

Varying how the children record their work is another useful way of breaking down some of that 'boxy' subject thinking. Using project books or portfolios means that any work related to the project is in one place. We use A4 books with the project question written on the front. We also invested in some of those fancy clear plastic covers that both protect the books and make them look important. Over the course of a term, because most work goes into the project book, they feel substantial. We've still got some separate subject books for discrete pieces of work, but it's the project books that the children care about the most – which is exactly the effect we're after.

A second issue that can crop up is the project losing its sense of enquiry as the work progresses. In a similar way to the problem of reverting to a subject-focused approach, this can stem from an overemphasis on getting through the content, and, as a result, defaulting to a model of delivering *at* the children rather than enabling them to influence the direction of the learning for themselves. Recording and displaying the children's thoughts and ideas that emerge from exploring and responding to the concepts is a good starting point, but this doesn't count for much if we plough on regardless, without paying any attention to what they are interested in.

Solving this problem requires bravery, because to do it successfully means we have to relinquish some control. Underpinning the curriculum with skills-based non-negotiables gives us some flexibility with content, and this can be applied both in the planning stages of projects and also as the projects develop.

For example, one of the projects the Year 6 children explored began with the question, 'How do we tell truth from tale?' Along with dealing with the concepts of 'belief', 'faith' and 'influence', this was a history-themed project and the teachers settled on Ancient China as the period to focus on. Before starting to think about how the project might evolve, they had a clear idea of the skills they wanted to develop over the course of the term thanks to the SOLO skills progression we looked at in Chapter 4.

Multistructural 	● *Recall* and place a range of relevant dates and events on a timeline. ● Recognise and *interpret* primary and secondary sources to find out about an aspect of the past. ● Use factual knowledge to *describe* past societies, periods and events. ● *Examine* and describe the beliefs, behaviour and characteristics of people from the past.
Relational 	● *Map* the current area of study on a timeline in relation to other studies. ● *Analyse* a range of primary and secondary sources to find out about an aspect of the past. ● Use factual knowledge to describe past societies, periods and events and begin to *make connections* between them. ● *Summarise* the beliefs, behaviour and characteristics of people, recognising difference in views and feelings.
Extended abstract 	● *Evaluate* the usefulness of primary and secondary sources and consider how conclusions were arrived at. ● Use a range of sources to *generalise* about an aspect of the past, suggesting omissions and the means of finding out missing information. ● *Elaborate* on factual knowledge when describing past societies, periods and events, making connections between them. ● Use evidence to *hypothesise* about the reasons for historical events, situations and the actions of individuals.

> ● *Appreciate* that aspects of the past – including beliefs, behaviour and characteristics – have been represented and interpreted in different ways, and give the reasons for this.

In terms of a starting point, there is enough here to give us real confidence that the children are going to develop the key historical skills we're interested in. And if we take the example we used earlier of working on primary and secondary sources, we can see that the skills are returned to frequently, with increasing depth, throughout the project. Along with confidence around skill coverage, the depth of knowledge the children will develop is inescapable. If we're developing the skill of using primary and secondary sources over and over again, then the range of knowledge grows too.

The level of rigour this gives us means that it's the perfect point at which to apply a layer of freedom and choice in terms of content. In the context of Ancient China, this meant that the teachers could allow the children to choose for themselves which particular parts of this period of history they wanted to learn about. Rather than give the children completely free rein, they were offered a range of areas to choose from, which included the Shang and Ming dynasties, the Terracotta Army, Taoism, Confucianism and Buddhism. From this broad selection, they picked the one that allowed them to explore the concept(s) that interested them the most and were then grouped according to their choice. The groups performed brilliantly because everyone shared the same interest. It also meant that, in most cases, the children worked with people they wouldn't usually work with, which added some variety.

On the face of it, teaching the children about different aspects of ancient China might seem like a logistical nightmare, but it was actually incredibly simple. The teachers taught skills, which were then applied to whichever area the children were working on. It didn't matter that one group were building their knowledge of Ming porcelain and another of Chinese mythology. They were all learning how to interpret primary and secondary sources of information (or whichever skill it was that they were targeting).

From the children's perspective, this felt like an incredible amount of choice and control; and the teacher could be pretty relaxed about it all because they knew exactly what the focus of the learning would be. The outcome of the project was an exhibition in which each group would take complete responsibility for the content and presentation of their artefacts and information. At the end of the term, when evaluating their project, one child fed back that the main reason they loved the project was because they had done everything for themselves and the teachers had done nothing! Actually, this couldn't be further from the truth, but perceptions are important, and by allowing choice in terms of the focus, the sense of independence that was clearly felt led to this incredibly empowering and motivating alternate reality.

This kind of flexibility around the context for the learning is a fairly familiar approach in the Early Years, and also one that's quite often misunderstood. If you really want to upset an Early Years teacher, the first thing to suggest is that all the children do is play all day. If you've still got your teeth, the next most frequently repeated assertion is that the Early Years is about letting the children decide for themselves what they're learning about. Both these statements are untrue. Early Years teachers have a very clear idea about what the children will be learning, but they have much more flexibility than most other teachers when it comes to context.

A great example of this cropped up a couple of years ago in a reception class. The teacher had decided to do a mini project on the Chinese New Year. (This was unconnected to the Ancient China project; it's just a coincidence – we're not obsessed!) To introduce the project to the children, she had transformed the role play area in the classroom into a Chinese restaurant, and, as it was the year of the dragon, she had created a papier mâché dragon's egg that the children would discover when they arrived. In terms of learning, the teacher wanted to explore writing lists, invitations, recipes and thank you notes by helping the children to plan a special event to celebrate the Chinese New Year.

The first session went well, and the children were as fascinated by the dragon's egg as she'd hoped. It turned out, though, that they were a bit too interested, and whenever she tried to broaden the conversation by making the connection to the idea of New Year, the children kept bringing it back to the egg. They wanted to know where it had come from. They were pretty confident that dragon's eggs don't just turn up out of the blue and had therefore decided that it must belong to someone important. It didn't take long before it was decided that it must be from the castle on the hill.[1]

As the teacher, you've got a couple of choices here. The first option is to decide that you're the one in charge and that, actually, you've heard enough of this kind of talk and it's time to get back to whatever's on the planning sheet. The second option is to go along with it and see what happens. The teacher decided to let the children run with it.

It turned out that the dragon's egg belonged to the prince and princess who lived in the castle (there was some disagreement over the exact ownership until the teacher helpfully suggested that perhaps it might belong to both the prince and princess on the grounds that they were twins). The children became obsessed with the castle, and very quickly the Chinese-themed role play area made way for a hastily constructed cardboard castle. It was a rush job, with lots of tape and marker pens, but the children helped out and they loved it.

After allowing the children to decide what they wanted the inside of the castle to look like (with the assistance of some carefully selected picture books), the children arrived in class one morning to find that a letter had arrived. The children knew instantly that it was important, largely because it looked very old (the teacher had been at it with the teabags). It was also rolled into a scroll, tied with gold ribbon and was sitting on a small velvet cushion in the middle of the classroom.

The children were pretty sure that the mysterious letter had come from the castle, and they wasted no time in getting the teacher to read it to them. They were right. It was from the queen. It turned out that it was the prince and princess's birthday, and the queen had decided that there should be a party to celebrate – the greatest party the kingdom had ever seen.

This almost tipped the children over the edge – they couldn't believe it and immediately started to talk about the kinds of things that should happen at a party. The teacher relied on Heathcote's technique of 'dropping to the universal' – safe in the knowledge that four-year-olds have better social lives than most adults and therefore have a massive amount of party-related experience on which

---

1   For the sake of clarity, this was an imagined castle (and hill). If you happen to work in a school that's within touching distance of an actual castle, then good for you. We're next door to some flats, so we have to think stuff up.

to draw. With very little persuasion, it was decided that the best way to record their ideas would be as a list. Following this, the children also thought that you would need invitations, and as there would be food to get ready, recipes would be useful too.

It won't have escaped your attention that these are exactly the same areas of learning that the teacher had intended to cover in the Chinese New Year project; nothing has really changed on the planning front, it's just the context that has shifted. There's no doubt that this approach takes some courage (i.e. not panicking and reverting to whatever you had in your head), but the rewards in terms of the children's motivation make it well worth while.

Along with being open to some flexibility in terms of context, to create a real sense of a developing and evolving project we can take a piece of helpful advice from the Reggio Emilia approach to Early Years practice.[2] One aspect of this philosophy focuses on the idea of 'emergent objectives'. What this basically boils down to is noticing things and making connections. This sounds like the easiest thing in the world, and it's what Early Years teachers are up to a lot of the time. For those brought up with strict messages about planning, though – and the resulting fear at the thought of deviating from the plan – it's not something we've really had time for.

Within any project, there will be occasions when other pieces of learning crop up. They won't be things that we've thought about beforehand, and they might involve a little detour. The first thing we need here is awareness. If we're so completely driven by the end goal or outcome, there will be no straying from the path because we won't even notice the emerging tangents when they appear. If we try to keep ourselves open to the possibility that something interesting, unexpected or useful might happen in the course of a project, then we've got a chance of not just seeing it, but also of connecting it to another aspect of learning or another part of the curriculum. Objectives like these can then be woven into the project, the children sense that they're not just going through the motions of a predetermined and rigidly planned topic, and a genuine sense of enquiry is embedded.

---

2   Reggio Emilia was developed by the Italian psychologist Loris Malaguzzi and is a child-centred approach to the curriculum that encourages the children to have an element of control over the direction of their learning. See P. Brunton and L. Thornton, *Bringing the Reggio Approach to Your Early Years Practice* (Abingdon: Routledge, 2010).

Phew.

So here it is, the first part of the book neatly summed up in less than fifty words:

Skills progression

(Sets out procedural knowledge, underpins learning and provides rigour.)

Content and concepts

(Determines propositional knowledge, adds relevance, creates connectedness and cohesion.)

Enquiry question

(Promotes curiosity and interest.)

Authentic outcomes and critical audience

(Builds motivation and raises expectations and expertise.)

Critique

(Enables the production of beautiful work.)

Job done (nearly) …

Part II:

PEDAGOGY

Everything we've looked at so far – from our 'less is more' philosophy through to an ethic of excellence – helps to create a clear structure and purpose for the curriculum, along with opening up the opportunity to develop those elusive personal learning and thinking skills we considered right at the start. It's about signalling our intent: this is what we believe curriculum is, this is what we want for our children and this is how we're going to make it happen.

We need this because without it, we're just floating around without any sense of where we're going or what we're aiming for. However, this clarity (whatever it looks like) won't make the blindest bit of difference if it doesn't actually filter down into our classrooms. A curriculum on paper isn't a curriculum, it's just a set of good intentions, and to bring it to life you need teachers.

Chapter 9

MONKEY SEX

I love a good documentary. It could be about almost anything – I'm not that fussy. I've watched programmes about emperor penguins, extreme caravanning, beetle fighting – they're all fascinating and perfect for whiling away time that should probably be spent on more important matters. My two girls, Eve and Imogen, love them too, which I'm really pleased about. It's good to do things as a family, and listening to Sir David Attenborough describing a day in the life of a whale means that two-thirds of the children are essentially taken care of for an hour without me having to break a sweat.

The documentary I'd come across on this particular occasion was set in the Amazon rainforest. This was an unusual piece of good luck because, unlike most other occasions, this actually bore some relevance to a topic that Eve was studying at school. The episode I'd recorded focused on a little gang of monkeys – in my opinion the best, and definitely the most entertaining, of all the animals.

After telling her about it, and waiting while she shot off upstairs to grab a notepad and pen, we sat down to watch. (I'd gathered up Imogen – who was about five at the time – en route to the sofa, so we were good to go.) It's hard to say exactly how long it was before things started to go wrong, but within about five minutes, I was thrust into what can only be described as a living nightmare.

Out of nowhere, and with absolutely no warning, we were faced with the most gratuitous monkey sex I've ever seen. Now, I was expecting the monkeys to be doing something, but I didn't think for a second that any self-respecting documentary maker would head into this particular dark corner of animal behaviour. It was incessant, and without even the slightest attempt to protect the monkeys' modesty with a soft-focus lens or the placement of a carefully positioned banana. The whole thing was played out in horrific high definition.

It turned out that the entire documentary was about the capuchin monkey mating season. As the action continued at pace in front of us, it wasn't long before their antics led to some pretty uncomfortable comments from the girls. Eve had now drawn up a fairly comprehensive series of notes ready to take into school for show and tell, and Imogen had suddenly decided that she had quite a lot of questions she'd like to be answered. Like any self-respecting dad under this kind of pressure, I decided to lie about what was happening on the screen and come up with different excuses to cover the monkeys' strange (yet undeniably impressive) performance. I couldn't turn it off, partly because the girls wouldn't let me and also because – in-between the bursts of monkey porn – there were some great little nuggets of information about the Amazon. And apparently, as we were about to find out – as well as being pretty active in the bedroom department – they are also one of the most intelligent troupes of monkeys on the planet.

After forty-five minutes, the mating season was finished and the documentary seemed to be winding down. Instead of packing up and heading home, though, the filmmakers had decided to put together one of those 'behind the scenes' segments, and within this was a moment that made the entire ordeal worthwhile.

Interested by just how intelligent the capuchin monkeys were, the scientists had decided to set them a test by creating a monkey-proof box. Inside the box was the monkeys' favourite snack (nuts), and to get at them they needed to press a lever on the front that released the nuts from a chute. Now, the monkeys were clever – they could use tools like sticks and rocks – but they'd never seen or used a lever before. With the box primed and ready, the scientists backed off to a safe distance and watched.

At first, what seemed like the whole troupe descended from the trees. The box was new and interesting and they wanted a look. Before long, the monkeys were attempting their tried-and-tested techniques for getting the job done. They sniffed, licked, nibbled, poked and smashed at the box with rocks. Nothing happened. After a while, they gave up and drifted back into the forest. Whilst all this was happening, one member of the troupe had been sitting to one side just watching. When the others had gone, he got up and went over to the box. After a few sniffs and a poke or two, he settled down in front of the box and looked at the lever. With his head cocked to one side, he reached out his hand, placed it on the lever and pressed. Immediately, the nuts tumbled down the chute. He couldn't believe his luck, and after a quick check to see that no one was looking, he ate them, and then pressed the lever again and again, each time getting more and more nuts.

When he'd had enough he toddled off into the trees and emerged a few seconds later with a friend. He brought him over to the box and showed him how it worked. After the excitement had died down, the friend was also at it with the lever, stuffing his face with nuts. Along with the entertainment factor that goes hand in hand with any animal-related problem-solving activity, what really stood out was the way in which the scientists summed up the success of this particular troupe of monkeys. They described them as having 'insatiable curiosity and the ability to learn from each other'.

As a teacher, this phrase struck me instantly, and hearing it made me think about my own two little monkeys, sitting either side of me on the sofa, still trying to get their heads around exactly what it was their dad was making them watch. They are both insatiably curious, but then most young people are.

In the Early Years, our youngest children get to have a go at the monkey-proof box on a daily basis. But as they get older, and as learning becomes more formal, we ditch the monkey-proofing for the path of least resistance – the clearest route from A to B – and their curiosity and creative thinking begin to fade. But what if it didn't? What if we kept hold of some of that monkeyness? The scientists didn't teach the monkeys to be curious or to think creatively, they just created the right conditions to draw it out. They could have simply put the nuts on a plate and left it in the clearing. The monkeys would have rolled up, eaten the nuts and then shuffled off home again. The outcome in both cases would have been the same. But thanks to the monkey-proof box, the journey to get there was harder, and the monkeys were pushed to test their curiosity and apply their creative thinking.

The box inspired curiosity because it was unusual. The challenge had purpose because it was real, and the process of learning was challenging. The curriculum we're generally faced with is nuts on a plate, but if we really want our young people to become the insatiably curious, independent, creative thinkers of tomorrow, this can't be the only thing we offer up. To give us a chance, we need a blended pedagogy – a range of strategies that allow us to create the conditions we need.

Before we get to the detail, it's worth defining exactly what approaches we're discussing:

- **Nuts on a plate**: Direct teaching – standing there and telling the children about stuff you know.

- **The monkey-proof box**: Throwing a spanner in the works, making life difficult and generally being disruptive (in the best possible sense of the word).

You could view these two methods as being at either end of a spectrum, but as with any spectrum, there are always things in-between. An example of exactly this kind of in-betweenness would be the idea of nuts scattered in a clearing. You're probably getting fed up with the nut analogy by now, but I need you to bear with me for just a while longer.

A nuts-on-a-plate approach can help us to efficiently build knowledge and skills (it's not the only way, but it's a good way). The monkey-proof box can help to elevate this by creating the conditions that will encourage the children to think differently. The last piece in this nut-themed jigsaw is to do with building independence. If we can scatter the nuts out there in the classroom, then the responsibility for finding them lies with the children – what I'd call facilitated learning. We need to make sure that the structures and means to learn are accessible, but the children have got to do it for themselves.

So, in a nutshell(!):

- **Nuts on a plate**: Direct teaching.

- **Nuts scattered in a clearing**: Facilitated learning – making the structures and means to learn accessible.

- **The monkey-proof box**: Creating and managing desirable difficulties, and regulating complexity and challenge.

Chapter 10
RAPID AND SUSTAINED NONSENSE

If you've never taught Year 1, then you're missing out. After stumbling through university and getting my first teaching job, this was exactly where I ended up. And within minutes, I knew it was the right place for me. The thing about Year 1 is that you don't have to try very hard. I know that's going to upset some people, and I'm not suggesting that Year 1 teachers don't try hard, but in terms of the reaction you get from the children you're pretty much sorted before you walk through the door. What I discovered is that Year 1 is as good as it gets. Pre-Year 1 is dominated by a few too many bodily fluids (mainly mucus), and post-Year 1 can be the start of a downward slope of children becoming cynical and world-weary.

Year 1 is the golden age of childhood. When you walk into a Year 1 classroom for the first time, the children look up at you in awe. You, their teacher, seem to be the single most important person in the universe – it's like the scene in *Return of the Jedi* with C-3PO and the Ewoks – you're a god amongst the little people. I'm not going to lie, I like a bit of adoration as much as the next man and I lapped it up. The children seemed to be constantly smiling and were desperate to please – if you needed a job doing, they'd be off like a shot and before you knew it, it was done. I think I spent more time thinking up little tasks for them to do than I did planning lessons.

It's easy to see why the Year 1 classroom is such a great place to teach – purely in terms of your own self-esteem it's a winner. But it's not necessarily the same in other parts of the school. And this came as something of a shock.

I first heard about my move to Year 6 via a phone call. All I had to do was cover the class for the day because the teacher was off ill and the head teacher was convinced that I was the right person for the job. Buoyed by my inflated sense of self-importance, I viewed this as being a fairly straightforward task. After all, Year 6 are just slightly taller versions of Year 1. I thought we'd just have a nice chat so I didn't plan much in advance. Because I was a young, cool-looking teacher, and also because of the fact that we were pretty close in age, I thought the conversation would flow fairly easily. As it turned out, it didn't.

Year 6 are not like Year 1. I think the main differences can be summarised in the following table:

Year 1	Year 6
They like you.	They don't like you.
They show you they like you.	See above.

This is a slight generalisation, but it seemed to me that the Year 6 children had forgotten the unspoken rule about the unconditional liking of teachers. What made this worse was that their teacher wasn't coming back any time soon, and by some pretty mean karma, I became the new Year 6 teacher by default. Not liking children is not a good thing for a teacher, and I was as unhappy about the situation as they were. I desperately wanted to get back to my lovely little Year 1s, but I was stuck with what appeared to be a class of angry young offenders.

I had an awful first term with them as I tried to get to grips with both their behaviour and the content that I had to teach them. I used certain strategies to help with this – in maths, I decided not to teach them any form of calculation, largely because it was quite hard. I had a vision of me turning my back (mistake number one) to do a sum on the board, only to get it wrong and then face humiliation. No chance, I wasn't going to touch anything more complex than number bonds to 10.

At the end of my first year, following this assessment tool called SATs that I'd only too late found out about, it turned out that this avoidance strategy hadn't worked that well. Without going into statistical detail, I hadn't covered myself in glory, and despite having a slightly better relationship with the children, I couldn't honestly say that their progress was anywhere close to what was expected.

Now, I might have been a rubbish teacher, but I wasn't one for giving up. Over the summer I decided to learn the stuff that I'd obviously not been taught myself whilst I was at school. I learnt about complex sentences and subordinate clauses. I learnt about angles, quadrilaterals, long division and all sorts of other complicated things. Perhaps unsurprisingly, it worked; things got better. The more I knew what I was talking about, the better it got.

Along with not wanting to be rubbish any more, the other source of encouragement came in the form of the shiny badges we could collect as teachers – in particular the 'outstanding' one. I desperately wanted the badge and, fortunately, we had a special checklist that told us how to get it. I think it was the ever helpful inspection people who originally invented it and there were lots of bullet points that we had to tick off to get to outstanding.

I would list them all, but I'm slightly worried about my word count so, in summary, here are some of the highlights:

- Write the learning objective and the date on the board (underlined and in cursive script for extra credit).
- Use a starter that requires focus and thinking skills.
- Use differentiated success criteria.
- Refer to the learning objective(s) consistently throughout the lesson.
- Check pupils' understanding using AfL (assessment for learning, in case you've forgotten).
- Be dynamic and enthusiastic.
- Have differentiated tasks (gifted and talented, SEN, EAL and any other groups you can think of).
- Cater for a wide range of learning styles – visual, auditory and kinaesthetic (the naughty ones who can only learn stuff by fiddling with things).

It was brilliant. Basically, you just ticked everything off and you were a nailed-on outstanding teacher. The only downside was that it was exhausting. Teaching outstanding lessons all the time was a bit of a burden, but having the badge made it all worthwhile. If someone important from the local authority turned up at school wanting a look around, I'd be rolled out. I'd turned myself from incompetent waffler into some kind of teaching machine.

There wasn't anything you could do to stop me – if you happened across my path, I made sure you were well and truly taught. If you had a question or if you put up your hand in my vicinity, I was all over it. I had the answers. If you were a child in my class, you'd go home exhausted from the sheer force of teaching that was flung in your direction.

After a while, though, I noticed that something was up. In my mind, there was absolutely no doubt that my teaching was spot on, but it slowly dawned on me that I hadn't fully considered the impact of my outstandingness on the children. The first time it happened was when I took a brief breather mid lesson. I don't know why I needed it; maybe all the progress that was happening had got to me, but the response from the children was interesting. They all stopped too. They looked confused at first, and then, as the silence continued, a sense of panic started to grip them. Some of them were looking at each other as if to say, 'Don't worry – he'll start up again soon.'

It seemed that when I wasn't leading the way with my usual dynamic and enthusiastic performance, the children were at a loss. They had become entirely dependent on me and whatever I was up to at the front. I'd become Mr Nuts-On-A-Plate, and even though I was serving up some pretty exciting nuts, there was no getting away from the fact that the children were being spoon-fed the curriculum.

This came as a blow, if I'm honest. The children always seemed to be having a good time, so I'd never really paused to think about what was actually going on. I felt guilty at first, but then decided that, actually, it wasn't my fault. I've already mentioned the outstanding checklists that were floating around in most schools, and the inspectors had a big part to play in these being used to make teachers deliver their lessons in a certain way. There were also other phrases being bandied around such as 'rapid and sustained progress' and 'pace'. At the time, we just accepted these things as part and parcel of what outstanding teaching was about, but, in hindsight, they are two of the most damaging concepts we've had thrown at us in recent times.

First of all, the idea that a lesson can result in rapid and sustained progress is just rubbish. You can't see progress (or, in fact, learning) in a single lesson; you can only see it over time. Ofsted seem to have finally caught up with this thinking and, to give them some credit, they have now changed their tune about how learning and progress are viewed. Pace is the unavoidable consequence of being told that the children have to make progress in a lesson. It does funny things to you as a teacher, and before you know it, you're belting your way through whatever bit of the curriculum it is at a hundred miles an hour.

It's important to point out that the problem isn't with the nuts-on-a-plate model of direct teaching, it's to do with how this is interpreted. I'm a huge fan of direct teaching, and using a blended pedagogy doesn't mean doing away with it, but it does mean we need to think about it differently. Nuts on a plate is an essential building block that will help us to explore thinking around building both independence and creative thinking, and without it, we're ignoring a significant part of our skill and expertise. But direct teaching has to be good, and by good, I mean clear and concise.

The effectiveness of modelling something for the children relies, to a massive extent, on the language we use. There is a whole section on language in my first book, *Guerrilla Teaching*, and if anything, I've become even more obsessed with it now that I've seen the impact it can have across an entire school.

Being able to boil a concept down to the key language is an essential skill for a teacher. There's so much we could say, but if we're not careful, it can easily become a jumble of closely related words and phrases. When you add into the mix the impact of children moving up from one year to the next, and with it the high likelihood that their new teacher will use different words and phrases to the teacher they had last year, then it's not a massive surprise that we often feel as if the children have forgotten lots of what they have supposedly been taught.

There are problems no matter where you look. In English, something as straightforward as a simple sentence can cause a problem. The most accurate way to define a simple sentence is to say that it consists of one (independent) clause and contains a subject and a verb. When children start working on simple sentences in Key Stage 1, the most commonly used explanation that I've seen involves the words 'noun' and 'verb'. Using this definition with the types of sentences children come across in reception and Year 1 seems to work fine, but the reason it's so important to use 'subject' and 'verb' instead isn't to do with what's happening now; it's to do with what will happen long after they've left your class. Having an eye on the bigger picture means recognising that, at a later date, they will be working on much more complicated sentence structures that are likely to contain several nouns, and being able to pick out which of them is the subject will make their life much easier in the long run.

Quite often as teachers, we get caught up with making sure our children understand whatever it is we're teaching them about in the moment, and as a result, we sometimes slip into saying things that make sense to the children now but will probably cause a problem later on. I had a conversation recently with some Year 1 teachers who obviously knew their stuff, and they started to talk about doing some 3D shape work with the children. One of the things that the children were struggling with was recognising the difference between 2D and 3D shapes. What the teachers went for in the end was that a 3D shape is a 'fat shape'. As soon as they said it to the children, they seemed to get it. It made sense to them and they happily went around the classroom finding examples. As a teacher, you'd be quite happy too. We set out to teach them something, they struggled to get it, we gave them an explanation and then the penny dropped.

If we're only interested in what happens in our own class, then everything's perfect. However, if we fast forward to some point in the not too distant future, they will be looking at 3D shapes again. When this happens, it's highly likely that the 'fat shape' definition used in Year 1 will be replaced with talk of dimensions – height, width and depth. If you then introduce the definition given to my eldest daughter in Year 7, that '3D shapes are shapes you can pick up', then it's not surprising that, in the children's brains, these various bits of language aren't automatically viewed as being related. Connections get missed and the potential to build on prior learning can be lost.

Getting over this problem needs a whole-school approach, which is not as difficult as it might seem. What if we just decided, as a school, that we were going to be prescriptive about certain key aspects of language within the curriculum? If we take writing as an example, in my opinion there are only three things the children need to have mastered to help them become great writers: simple, compound and complex sentences. Of course there are other objectives in the curriculum, and they will need to learn some of that to pass a test, but in terms of actually producing brilliant writing, we focus on just those three sentence types.

Now that we've narrowed it down and marginalised some of the other grammatical nonsense (active and passive voice, expanded noun phrases, fronted adverbials – take your pick!), it's not a stretch to come up with a school-wide agreement on how we define and explain each sentence type. What this gives us is children moving from one class to the next and hearing the stuff that matters the most being presented in exactly the way that they've heard before.

If we applied the same process to maths, then looking at the language we use for something as vital as place value would be a good place to start. What happens to a number when we multiply it by 10? Add a zero? Move the decimal place one place to the right? Move the digits one place to the left? In maths, it's more black and white than in English – there's a right way and a wrong way, so when we've found our language, we just decide that that's what everyone will use and then stick to it.

This has had a massive impact on both children with SEN and those with EAL. If we're a lot clearer with our language (and therefore more consistent with its repetition), then it's obviously going to benefit the children who may experience processing difficulties (we'll talk more about cognitive load later in this chapter), and it will definitely benefit the acquisition of new language for those trying to learn it for the first time. I've done lots of training as a teacher on both EAL and SEN, and the thing that always struck me most is that what is deemed *good practice for these groups is actually good practice for all children*.

Beyond English and maths, we could apply this to history, geography, the arts and design technology, or any other subject for that matter – and thanks to the skills progression we looked at earlier, we're already halfway towards clarifying the language we'd need. If we take the SOLO verbs 'interpret', 'analyse' and 'generalise', it makes sense that these words are always defined in the same way, and whilst the exact wording doesn't really matter, having collective agreement across a school does:

- **Interpret**: Explain the meaning of …
- **Analyse**: Examine methodically and in detail …
- **Generalise**: Make a statement based on facts …

There are different ways of developing this consistency. We could decide as a school that nailing down language will be the main focus – one of those school priorities or targets that we have to have. What if, instead of the usual organisational stuff we get bogged down with in staff meetings, we dedicate the first ten minutes each week to clarifying language for one key piece of learning? It's such a simple thing yet the impact could be huge. What it also does is open our eyes to what's happening across other years in school. As teachers, we can get slightly insular in our own year groups, and thanks to the lingering threat of 'rapid and sustained progress', we're only focused on what we can achieve in sixty-minute blocks. If we're genuinely interested in learning, though, we need to forget the quick-fix stuff and start thinking about the long haul.

This all seems a long way from being the basis for developing a creative curriculum, but establishing solid foundations like this is essential. It's easy to get distracted by the interesting, creative aspects of learning and teaching, but if we're adopting a 'creativity with rigour' approach to the wider curriculum through our focus on skills, then it makes sense that we follow the same path when it comes to the detail of learning.

Chapter 11

NUTS ON A PLATE

A traditional lesson always starts with the teaching bit. Adding rigour and consistency of language to this will improve the quality of teaching no end, but there's still another problem for us for us to get to grips with – planning.

Planning was easy when I first started teaching because of the four-part lesson rule. We had a ten-minute warm-up, a twenty-minute teaching bit, twenty minutes of independent work and then ten minutes to wrap things up with a plenary. In the twenty-minute teaching bit we modelled whatever it was we wanted the children to learn. Several times. We did this for a couple of reasons. First, we had to fill the time somehow, and we couldn't move on to the next section of our lesson before the time was up. That was the law. The second reason was differentiation.

I've been having a go at differentiation for most of my career, despite having the sneaking suspicion that it was a waste of time. I should clarify this: I wholeheartedly believe that we should be meeting the needs of our learners and that appropriate scaffolding and support should be given where needed. Differentiation – or, more specifically, what it's come to mean – is something very different.

The way that most of us were taught to differentiate was to pitch learning to the middle ability children in the class, and then differentiate up for the more able/ higher attaining/clever kids, and differentiate down for the less able/lower attaining/lemons group. This meant that any modelling we did was aimed at the (hopefully) biggish middle ability group, although we probably tended to go for the lower end of this group – just to make sure they got it.

The other two groups weren't really a concern. The more able ones could probably do it already and the lower ability ones had a teaching assistant with them who, if they waited long enough, would do it for them. Almost every lesson operated like this. Twenty minutes of teaching followed by differentiated independent activities.

The first problem with this is to do with expectation. Traditional differentiation places a fixed ceiling on what the children can achieve. Over the years, it's meant we've developed tasks and activities that different groups could cope with, whilst any form of challenge was reserved for the most able in the class. Some children have spent their entire school life on the lemons table, bouncing from one intervention to the next, glued to the trusty teaching assistant.

I think that the most surprising thing about all of this is probably just how long it took most of us to realise that it doesn't work – for any of the children involved. It's pretty obvious that it's not helpful for the more able learners. They have to sit, bored, listening to an explanation of something they can do in their sleep. The lower ability kids aren't getting a great deal out of it either. They might not be getting the content if it's pitched above their heads, but even if they did, it's irrelevant because the activity they've been given has been simplified to such a degree that it doesn't bear much relation to what has been spoken about anyway.

The one group that this style of teaching should be helping are the middle ability ones, but I'm not even convinced that this is happening effectively. This is how modelling usually happens: we start to explain the concept or process. After one or maybe two examples, we'll have a look for any flicker of recognition in the faces of the children. When I say children, what I really mean is the middle ability children (lower end). They're the ones that this is really aimed at, so we're looking to them for some feedback. A few of them might be nodding along, seeming to get it, but we haven't got enough of them yet, so we do another example and explain it again. We check again for evidence of it being understood. There's still a couple of unsure faces – OK, we'll do just one more.

Before we know it, we've been there for twenty minutes making sure they 'feel' ready to get on with their independent work. On reflection, this isn't about how they feel – it's about how *we* feel. How confident are we in the children's ability to do the thing we want them to do? Given our understandable nervousness around the whole progress issue, this means we're likely to edge more towards the 'pretty certain' end of the spectrum when gauging their readiness to do whatever it is we're after.

This will work for some children but that doesn't mean it's desirable – in fact, we're just back to the familiar problem of creating passive learners who just sit and wait for the teacher to do all the hard work for them. Along with sapping the children's independence, there's also the high probability that for particular children it's actually doing more harm than good – something I hadn't really considered until a conversation I had with my youngest daughter.

Imogen is eleven years old and has the most amazing brain. She is creative, imaginative and relentlessly curious. As part of this incredible set-up, she also has some traits that are frequently associated with dyslexia. One of the ways this impacts her is to do with cognitive load (the amount of mental effort going on in the working memory). If we look at working memory as a shelf, when several things are added in one go, the odd bit will fall off the edge. This kind of difference in processing is not uncommon in our classrooms and it frequently goes unnoticed due to the coping strategies that children develop.

Imogen would sit somewhere in the middle of the group that our 'differentiated' lesson was supposed to target. If you were Imogen's teacher, hers is one of the faces you'd have an eye on when deciding whether it was sinking in or not. Her thoughts on being 'taught' were fascinating. In talking about her learning, her overriding feeling was that she wished her teacher would just let her 'get on'. She went on to explain that when the teacher modelled whatever it was, she got some of it the first time. But just as she was trying to process it, the teacher interrupted her thinking with another example, then possibly interrupted again with yet another. Essentially, while Imogen was trying to concentrate on the information she'd been given, the teacher was making noise. By the end of it, she was often more confused than she was at the start.

Over-modelling is an incredibly easy trap to fall into as a teacher, and it isn't necessarily improved by shifting from a differentiated model to a 'mastery' approach. I'll talk more about mastery in Chapter 15, but for now, the key difference between mastery and differentiation is a shift in expectation. With mastery, we're aiming much higher than before and then thinking about how we can support, structure and scaffold all of our children to get there. In principle, it's long overdue and immediately does away with the limitations that are imposed through ability grouping. But over-modelling can potentially make this process doubly difficult for the children. Before we were over-modelling something that wasn't that hard in the first place, but now we're aiming for something that's potentially much more difficult – and with it comes the temptation to go for even more examples than before.

Whether it's differentiation or mastery, to avoid going around in circles, we need to accept that our understanding of the cause-and-effect relationship between teaching and learning is not as clear-cut as we thought, and the perfect place to begin is by questioning some of the long-established beliefs that have come to shape our classroom practice.

Chapter 12

NUTS SCATTERED IN A CLEARING

One of the things we've been experimenting with for a while now is what happens if we stop with the over-modelling. To help with this, we asked the following question: 'What if, for any given piece of learning, you were only allowed to model it once?' Now, this isn't a rule, it's just something to try – a challenge, I suppose.

What it does to you as a teacher is interesting. All of a sudden there's a bit of pressure. If you've only got one shot at it, it's got to be right. It forces you into thinking really carefully about how you'll explain it, which, in turn, automatically sharpens up your language. Knowing that we can always go over something again if they don't get it can make us sloppy, besides, a little jeopardy keeps things interesting.

In terms of the children, it definitely helps the more able lot. Previously they had to hang around until we'd finished with our multiple examples before being allowed to get on. Now, they might have to listen to it once – which, if nothing else, will help to clarify their thinking or clear up a misconception – and then it's only a matter of minutes before they're let loose and can get stuck in. The other children are now a problem, though, because for lots of them, modelling once might not be anywhere near enough.

To pick this problem apart, the first thing we need to address is our understanding of what the word 'modelling' means. To me, possibly because of how I was trained, I always associated it with the thing that I did at the front of the class. Modelling was basically me teaching. What happened after that was that the children got to practise and apply it through a range of different activities. In hindsight, this is a limited way of viewing modelling. I'd only ever treated it as a verb and hadn't considered for a second that 'model' could also be a noun.

The realisation that modelling is not restricted to the things that come out of my mouth was a revelation. Like most aspects of good practice in education, I first saw effective examples of this in the Early Years. Teaching in the Early Years is tough, but it is also possibly the very best place in school to be working if you're interested in seeing up close what learners look like. One of the challenges we face with very young children is how to get them to do a particular activity without having an adult there to guide them through it. This, in a nutshell, is the reason why the idea of continuous provision terrifies anyone who has never had to do it.

In a great Early Years setting, continuous provision consists of a constant, high quality and stimulating environment that allows children to explore, whilst also offering them the opportunity to challenge their learning and thinking. However, simply providing this environment isn't enough; if we just stepped back and left the children to it, our carefully designed lesson would quickly descend into chaos. To avoid this, the adults play an important role in skilfully and subtly guiding, nudging, prompting and questioning the children so that opportunities are maximised. In addition to this, and to address the fact that an adult can't do this at all times and in all places, another layer of support is frequently added in the form of worked examples. I've never heard a foundation teacher actually describe what they do as using a 'worked example', but this is exactly what they are.

As children get older, the processes they need to go through for lots of aspects of the curriculum get more complicated. To avoid reacting to this by simply throwing more and more stuff at the working memory, we can take on board some lessons from cognitive load theory, which was developed in the late 1980s thanks to a study by the educational psychologist John Sweller.[1] The main thinking is that cognitive load can be reduced by the way in which instruction is designed. One of the ways of doing this is through the use of worked examples – essentially another means of modelling without us having to open our mouths.

In the Early Years, I've seen some brilliant visual worked examples used to help children independently access a whole range of different provision without the need for endless repetitive modelling from the teacher. In one phonics-based activity that was about building CVC words (consonant, vowel, consonant for those unfamiliar with early phonics), the worked example consisted of a series of photographs. In the first picture there was a hand reaching into a pot to pick out the first phoneme, 'r'. The second picture showed this being repeated to form the word 'r-i-p'. The third photo showed the hand holding a pointer and using it to pick out the corresponding phonemes on a sound chart. The final picture went back to the disembodied hand again and showed it pointing to each phoneme in the word to read it aloud. Now, for this to work, it had to be modelled by an adult

---

1   See J. Sweller, P. Ayres and S. Kalyuga, *Cognitive Load Theory* (New York: Springer, 2011).

at the start of the process. After this, thanks to the way the worked example had been put together, the children were able to use the visual cues to access the task by themselves.

As tasks become more complicated, worked examples are used to scaffold and support the process, meaning there's much less for children to hold in their working memory and more opportunity for them to process information at their own speed.

Whenever I spend time in the Early Years and see stuff like this working, I'm caught between feeling totally amazed that four-year-olds can operate independently like this, and then completely frustrated that older children can't. However, taking this one aspect of Early Years practice and spreading it as widely as possible through school can go a long way towards solving this problem.

Getting a worked example just right puts us under the same kind of pressure as only having one shot at saying something to the children. And if knowing we're only going to say something once makes us focus more intently on the language we use, then creating a worked example has the same effect from a visual perspective.

Using visuals has always been a big part of teaching, but if we could only give the children one example of a particular piece of learning or process, what would it look like?

One of the most exciting moments in my teaching career came with the delivery of the school's very first interactive whiteboard. It's hard to explain what this was like to younger teachers who've grown up with this kind of technology, but for someone who was used to coping with marker pens and a wobbly, standy-uppy, three-legged, old-school whiteboard, it was a massive leap forwards. All of a sudden, I had a pen that could write on a virtual page. It was like magic. I wrote, drew and scribbled with an incredibly clever piece of plastic and it appeared digitally. And as if this wasn't enough, I then discovered the fancy bits – the software that came with the board had built-in clip art, sound effects and animations. There were huge resource banks covering almost every possible image you could ever need, and also a handy screen capture tool to add in that picture from the internet of a juggling camel that you knew would make all the difference to your maths lesson.

I absolutely loved it. Lesson planning evolved into creating page after page of digital flipcharts. Page one was your learning objective, but with a clip art palm tree background to make it more exciting. Page two was probably a list of success criteria, but with a shape covering them up so I could dramatically reveal them one by one. Page three would have been the start of some teaching – maybe the first example of whatever I was intending to do, obviously accompanied by a funny-looking wizard in the bottom corner (because everyone likes magic) and a chimp with a speech bubble that included some questions I'd thought up.

I threw everything at the flipcharts – there was no clip art known to man that I couldn't shoehorn into a lesson, and I did it because I thought it made things more stimulating for the children. And it worked, at least to begin with. In truth, they were only impressed for a day or two. It really annoyed me how quickly they started to take the new technology for granted – there was the initial buzz, but after that they weren't overly impressed that I could hide words under a shape. They weren't even that bothered about my chimp.

At the height of my clip art addiction, I probably went way beyond engagement and headed firmly into distraction. There's nothing wrong with adding something visually appealing or interesting to a plain slide or flipchart page, but the moment it interferes with or detracts from whatever it is we're supposed to be explaining, it needs to stop.

The design and layout of the visual side of our modelling is especially important if we're going to use it not only to teach from, but also to support and scaffold the children when they begin to work independently. Fortunately, instead of having to do more, this usually involves the process of stripping stuff back.

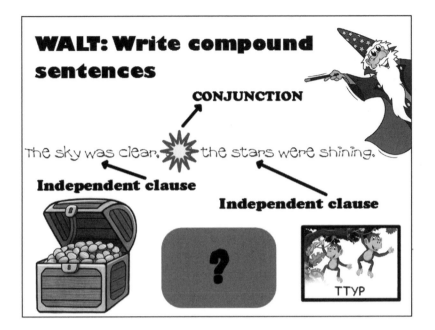

Version 1 (*c.* 2006–2011)

As you can see in the example above, the wizard has made an appearance, there are some fancy fonts, there's probably something pretty exciting hiding underneath the treasure box (like a range of alternative conjunctions), and the chimps are there as a reminder that I want the children to talk about a particular point. There's a lot going on, and exactly what the children will focus on is anyone's guess.

If we get rid of the distracting bits and think more carefully about the best possible way to present this information, we might end up with something more like this:

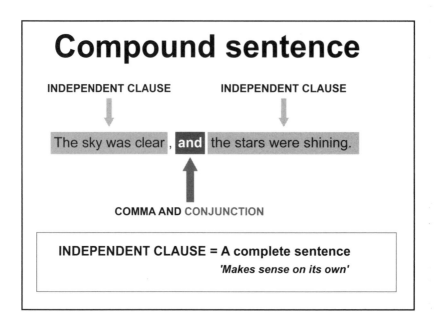

Version 2: modern-day classroom

This is stating the obvious, but there are a couple of useful visual things going on here that enhance rather than detract from the point. First of all, the conjunction 'and' is in blue. (Now, you'll have to trust me on this and use your imagination because the printing budget wouldn't stretch to colour – we blew it all on copyright payments for the wizard.) The reason for this is because, in my school, coordinating conjunctions are always blue and subordinating conjunctions are always yellow – from Year 1 (or whenever the children are ready for them to be introduced) all the way through to Year 6. This isn't a grammar rule, it's our rule. The choice of colours is irrelevant – the important bit is that they're consistent year after year. The independent clauses are presented in blocks, and while I'm not trying to say that this is the definitively right way to present compound sentences, for us it builds on the children's prior understanding about the unit of a simple sentence. All we're doing here is joining two of those units together.

I know there will be some people out there who might accuse me of stripping the fun out of teaching, but if we're relying on clip art and fancy fonts to show off our personality and engage our children, then we're in trouble. This is about learning, and making sure that the visual representation of that learning is as clear as possible.

Now that we've thought about exactly what it will look like, we've not only clarified our teaching but we've also ended up with a ready-made worked example that can be used as our first layer of support. We now need to think about how exactly it's going to be used.

If we've reduced our modelling to its simplest and most concise form, then we're also reducing the certainty that the children will be able to do what we want them to do. The idea of uncertainty is an important one. Worked examples are not just a nice bit of support for a few children who might not be able to keep up, and they completely lose their usefulness if we slip back into those over-modelling habits we discussed earlier. The ideal situation is to create the conditions in which *most* of the children will need them.

This involves risk, but by embracing the uncertainty that comes from limiting our modelling, we can ensure that the process of learning is much more effective for everyone involved. We're reducing the time wasted for the children who've picked it up quickly, managing cognitive load to help with processing and, thanks to our modelling being only the start of the process, we're shifting responsibility for continuing the learning to the children. The worked example reinforces our modelling and gives them everything they need in order to be successful, but they've got to think hard about it and do it for themselves.

It goes without saying that the compound sentence example would only be introduced when the children have mastered simple sentences, so thanks to the teaching and the worked example, they should all be able to write a compound sentence by the end of the lesson.[2] In terms of the outcome, we can look at this

---

2   Some people believe that mastery is about ensuring, and in some cases insisting, that all children reach a particular level or produce exactly the same thing. This is wrong. We work with high numbers of children with exceptional needs at our school and some are cognitively unable to perform at age-related expectations. This doesn't mean that we have lower expectations for them or that they can't be as successful as anyone else – it just means that success looks different. A sentence doesn't have to be written with words for it to be a sentence – it could be recorded using images or symbols (e.g. Communicate: In Print – a symbol-supported desktop publishing programme) or it could be spoken and recorded using a Talking Tins lid (a piece of plastic the size of an ice hockey puck that records and plays back speech at the touch of a button). Expecting all children to produce or reach an identical outcome isn't (or shouldn't be) what mastery is about.

in one of two ways: either 'That's brilliant, they've got it, let's move on' or rec-ognise it for what it really is – a good start.

There won't be many of us out there who haven't experienced the situation in which we've taught a class something and it's gone pretty well. The children can reel off whatever it is we've done with them – it's a complete success. But when returning to it the next day or the next week (following a sleep), it appears that they have no real idea of what we're talking about.

The problem is that they didn't actually learn it in the first place. Using a detailed worked example, like our compound sentence one, means the children are able to perform during the course of a lesson. This is important, but it's not the same as learning. If a child has learnt something then it has to be properly embedded. There will be a change in long-term memory – they are now able to do some-thing they couldn't do before. Can we be sure that they will they still be able to do it in a week's time? What about in a month? And, perhaps most importantly, can they do it without support?

Worked examples are great, but they're a means to an end. Ultimately, I don't want the children to need them at all, because this will signify that they have remembered for themselves and can apply the skill completely independently. What this means, in terms of the learning process, is that whilst it's useful to start with high levels of scaffolding and support, to shift from performance to learning we need to think about how to wean them off it.

This is a simple process now that we've got a starting point. The initial worked example represents the most support that can be given. To create a stage with slightly less support, and then another with less again, really just means reducing the information to which the children have access. As support is reduced, the children have to work harder and harder at remembering and applying the pro-cess until the examples are no longer needed.

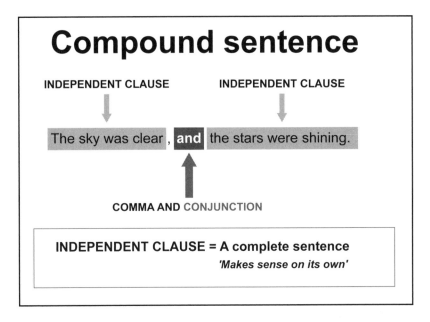

Worked example 1: high support

A bit less:

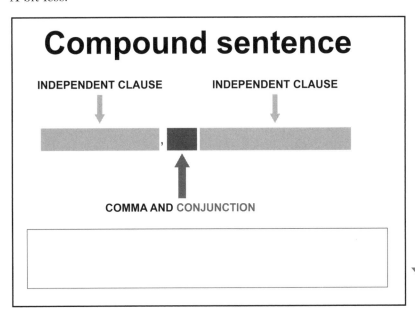

PERFORMANCE

A bit less again:

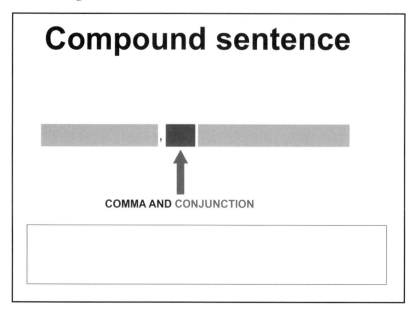

Virtually nothing:

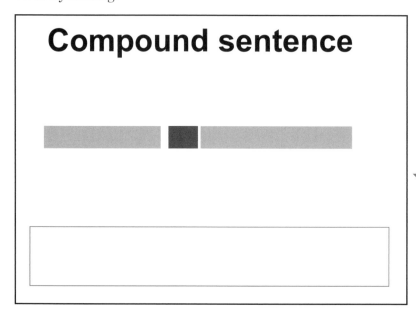

LEARNING

Thanks to my handy flipchart (other modelling products are available), once I've created the first example to share with the children, the other versions are just duplicated with increasing amounts of stuff deleted. Not only is this quick to do, but a set of well-designed worked examples means that your planning is done and dusted.

It's worth bearing in mind that this is just my thinking around how to develop this one piece of learning with a particular group of children. You might decide that not all the stages are necessary or you could decide to remove the support in slightly different ways. The timing of this removal is also completely dependent on the children – we might be talking days, weeks or even months. For example, if I was a Year 3 teacher focusing on compound sentences, then I might be thinking about the weaning happening over the course of a couple of terms or maybe even a year.[3] If it was older children, the time frame might be reduced.

Regardless of what they look like or how we use them, the most important thing about worked examples is that they're not going to be given to specific children or groups of children based on any notion of ability. These faded worked examples are for anyone and everyone. Working in this way allows the children to decide for themselves which layer of support they need. For some, it might be the highly scaffolded example that mirrors exactly the modelling we've just done. They can pick one up and, in their own time, use it to independently access the learning. Others might choose not to use them at all and just get going straight from the off. Along with the self-selection of the starting point, the children can also control how and when to reduce the support they need. As they start to tackle the learning, there might be some practice using high support. A couple of sessions later might see them drop a layer or two as they gradually push themselves to remember and apply more and more of the process for themselves.

In developing this idea, we also made use of a handy app to digitalise the whole process. ShowMe is available for free, and if you have access to tablets it adds

---

3   Before I have a whole load of Year 3 teachers shouting at me about the fact that the children should be doing much more than compound sentences in their lessons, it's worth thinking about what would happen if we just ignored the objectives that are laid out in the curriculum document and focused on the stuff that matters instead. Many Year 4 teachers would bite your hand off if children came to them having mastered simple and compound sentences to the point that they could use them in any given piece of writing without any scaffolding or support. In the big scheme of things, the children would still have three years to get to grips with complex sentences, but they'd be doing it with a much firmer foundation.

another dimension to the usefulness of worked examples. It's basically a blank whiteboard page that you can write on but with the advantage of being able to record your annotations and also add a voiceover. The presentations work brilliantly for maths when you're modelling a process that might be complex or has lots of steps. When you've recorded your modelling you can save it and link it to a QR code which makes it instantly accessible in the classroom.[4]

Admittedly, I've made this sound pretty straightforward, but it would be dishonest if I didn't mention the afternoon I wasted making a ShowMe tutorial about non-defining relative clauses. My first mistake was thinking that non-defining relative clauses are that important. My second was thinking that I knew what one was. Again, it goes back to the clarity and conciseness of language that I've already touched on. I thought I knew it, but that was nowhere close to being good enough. It took about six or seven takes before I was happy, but, on reflection, a much better use of my time would have been to make a presentation on a part of the curriculum that actually mattered.

The advantages definitely outweigh the pain you might have to endure to make a tutorial, though. The first thing it does is sharpen up your language – it might require a few takes, but it's got to be better to iron this out in private instead of stumbling through it in front of the children. Second, when it's done, and you're happy with what you've recorded, then you've got it forever. If you're the generous type, you can share it with colleagues in the hope that they share theirs with you. There's not a huge difference between the Year 1 and the Year 2 curriculum – or 3 and 4 or 5 and 6 – so by deciding on some key bits of learning you'd like to focus on, and then sharing it out between a few classes, you can actually build a decent library without working yourself into the ground.

In terms of practicalities, along with having some visual worked examples scattered around the room, we can also add in some QR codes and a few tablets. One of our Year 6 girls made amazing use of this technology over the course of some learning about rounding decimal numbers using a number line. The class teacher had gone through the process of deciding exactly how she was going to model the concept, she had created her highly scaffolded worked example and also a ShowMe with QR code which the children could access on a tablet with headphones.

---

4 If you've never used a QR code before, there are lots of websites out there that will create them for you for free – all you'll need to do is paste in the URL and you're good to go. Try googling 'QR generator', pick a site and have a go!

On day one of the learning, the teacher modelled the method for rounding once for the children, and then allowed them to select the support/scaffolding they felt would best support them with the learning. The girl in question went straight for a QR code, got a tablet and plugged herself into the headphones. She kept pausing the tutorial to complete part of the rounding process in her book, before unpausing and watching/listening to a little bit more. At the end of the session, thanks to countless repeated views of the clip she could do the rounding and had got everything right (a good start!). Day two began with the pupil going back to the tablet again, but this time she decided not to wear the headphones. Again, she was successful, but without the need for her teacher's audio commentary. Day three – again she went for the tablet, but placed it close by on the table, and only gave it the briefest of glances to remind herself that she was doing the right thing. On day four, she didn't bother with the tablet at all.

Without any involvement from her teacher, this young girl had decided how best to wean herself off the support. The self-management involved in this is huge, and for this pupil in particular, it meant that she was able to access a piece of learning that, had she been stuck in an ability group with a differentiated task, she would never have been given in the first place.

Along with using different forms of worked examples, there are also the adults in the room to think about, and we'd be daft to ignore the support/guidance/ challenge that teachers and teaching assistants can bring to the party. Organising this is pretty straightforward, but rather than attaching an adult to the lower ability children, we can apply the same idea of self-selection that we've looked at already.

One of the first things we did was to set up a 'support table'. The idea was that it would be manned by an adult and open to anyone. If a child wanted to drop in, then they could – the support would be there. In Key Stage 1, this was massively popular – the children loved the support table and would jostle to get closest to the adult. In Key Stage 2, nobody liked the support table. If a pupil even drifted close to it they became a social outcast. After trying a few different adults at the table just to check that it wasn't personal, it became obvious that it was the word 'support' they didn't like. The children didn't want to be seen to need support, even if they knew they could really do with it. Fortunately, the solution to this was incredibly easy – we just stopped calling it a support table and called it a 'workshop' instead. Dropping into a workshop was no problem at all – it became socially acceptable.

(This might seem hard to believe, but you do get the odd occasion where the innocence/naivety of young people plays right into your hands.)

What this didn't solve was the difficulty of it being too popular, particularly with the younger children. To get over this, we decided to add in a time delay: 'OK children, a workshop will be starting over here in five minutes' time – if you want to drop in you're more than welcome. Five minutes' time …' What this did immediately was to force the children out into the classroom to have a go for themselves. And what they found scattered out there were lots of things that could help. If they found that the worked examples, practical resources, manipulatives, reference books, dictionaries or whatever else didn't help, then they only had to struggle for a limited time before the workshop began – which in itself is no bad thing.

The five minutes doesn't need to be five minutes – it could be three or ten. What matters is that the children are encouraged/pushed into having a go. For some of them, their reluctance to try something isn't entirely their fault. There will be some who've been sitting with a teaching assistant since reception, and they've come to believe that they can only be successful with support because they've spent their life in interventions or groups that reinforce this thinking. Syphoning children off into these kinds of groups can sometimes do more harm than good. If the children can be supported in class, then they should be supported in class.

Creating multilayered support is a much better way to think about differentiation. A mastery approach doesn't mean we just ignore the needs of our children and expect them all to be successful through sheer force of will or by telling them to have a 'growth mindset'[5] or 'grit'.[6] The support, structure and scaffolding still needs to be there, but helping the children to take responsibility for managing this process for themselves represents a significant shift in the ownership of learning and the re-emergence of their independence. This has had a massive impact on our children. Although to begin with we'd still have some who would tell us they didn't know what to do, a quick nudge from the teacher in the direction of a worked example soon made them realise that the nuts they needed were out there – they just had to get them for themselves.

---

5 For more on growth and fixed mindsets see C. S. Dweck, *Mindset: Changing the Way You Think to Fulfil Your Potential* (London: Robinson, 2017).

6 A. L. Duckworth, Grit: The Power of Passion and Perseverance [video], *TED.com* (2013). Available at: https://www.ted.com/talks/angela_lee_duckworth_grit_the_power_of_passion_and_perseverance/.

Chapter 13

ACROSS THE CURRICULUM

Foundation subjects have had a tough time over recent years, thanks largely to the obsession with English and maths. I've never met anyone who has set out to provide their children with a narrow and unbalanced curriculum, but there's no doubt that the pressure to hit data targets has led to schools prioritising core subjects over everything else.

By creating long-term projects, we've had the opportunity to raise the profile of these subjects by giving them the space and time they deserve. To really highlight their importance, though, we can go further and apply exactly the same thinking that we've employed in the English and maths examples to the rest of the curriculum.

Let's start with the history skills from Chapter 4:

- **Multistructural**: Recognise and *interpret* primary and secondary sources to find out about an aspect of the past

- **Relational**: *Analyse* primary and secondary sources to find out about an aspect of the past.

- **Extended abstract**: Use a range of sources to *generalise* about an aspect of the past, suggesting omissions and the means of finding out missing information.

The actual differences between the statements are quite subtle as the complexity increases, so, again, if we're not careful, it could just end up being one of those important-sounding curriculum documents that we like to have on file even though it's not of any proper use. To get around this, and to give us the best possible chance of creating something that actually helps both us and the children, there are ways in which we can make this more explicit.

The first thing to think about is how we're going to define the words we're interested in. At the risk of stating the obvious, it's relatively easy to arrive at the kind of clear and concise statements we're after by first looking up the SOLO verbs in a dictionary, and then thinking about which definition would work best with the children:

- **Interpret**: Explain the meaning of.
- **Analyse**: Examine methodically and in detail.
- **Generalise**: Make a statement based on facts.

With the definitions worked out, we can then start to think about what the development of a particular skill would look like in reality, and for this, some simple visuals could be used to prompt or support:

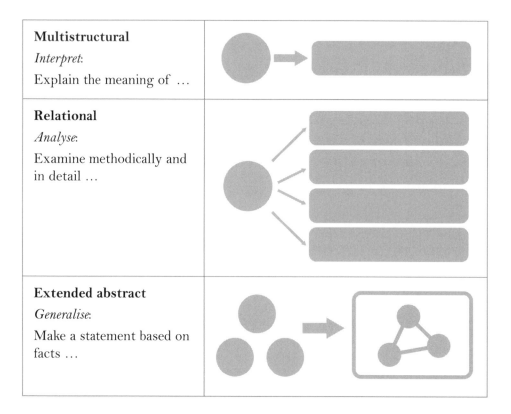

Multistructural *Interpret*: Explain the meaning of …	
Relational *Analyse*: Examine methodically and in detail …	
Extended abstract *Generalise*: Make a statement based on facts …	

It wouldn't take forever to create similar visuals for other SOLO verbs. In fact, if we picked another three, say 'consider', 'summarise' and 'elaborate', I bet it would take you no longer than five minutes to come up with some sketches of your own.

This additional layer could be viewed as being non-essential, but what it does is clearly signal our intent. We're not interested in having a skills-based curriculum just to feel good about ourselves, and we don't want it to be just a 'nice idea' that only exists on paper. If we're going to do it, then it needs to be done properly. We want skills that show clear progression through the school; skills that inform planning and skills that are carefully crafted so they can be used as a formative assessment tool which gauges depth of understanding rather than simply coverage. Above all else, we want skills that actually translate directly into classroom practice.

If we focus on the word 'analyse', it won't have escaped your notice that it shares a lot of the visual qualities that we'd be looking for in a worked example. It's simple, straightforward and easily understandable as a concept. Without doing anything, it would represent the lowest level of support and scaffolding and would be of most use as a visual prompt or cue when the children have more or less learnt how to do the thing we want them to do.

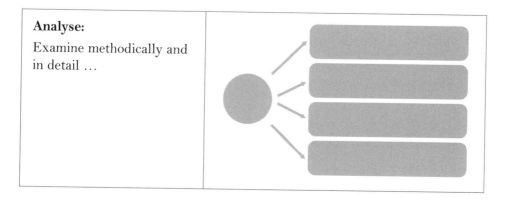

Analyse:

Examine methodically and in detail …

To give us the first layer of high scaffolding and high support that would help at the start of the learning process, we just need to go back and fill in some of the detail.

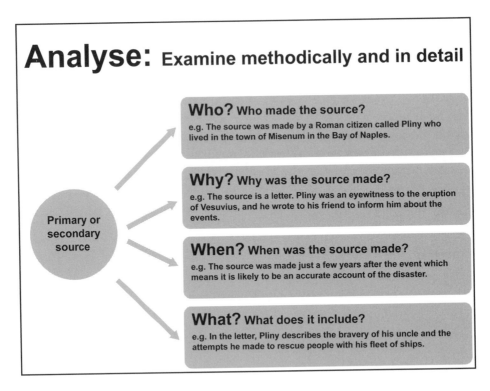

Worked example 1: high scaffolding

Just like the other worked examples we've explored, the detail is essentially our modelling, so along with us having a clear idea about what this skill looks like, it also gives us the means of extending the modelling in a way that shifts the focus from the teacher to the learner. The fact that it's about the eruption of Mount Vesuvius is irrelevant because what we're really after is for the children to apply it to whatever knowledge they're working on at that particular time.

And for the sake of completion, once we've created the first layer, we can then play around with the idea of faded worked examples to reduce the support as children remember, internalise and understand more and more of the process.

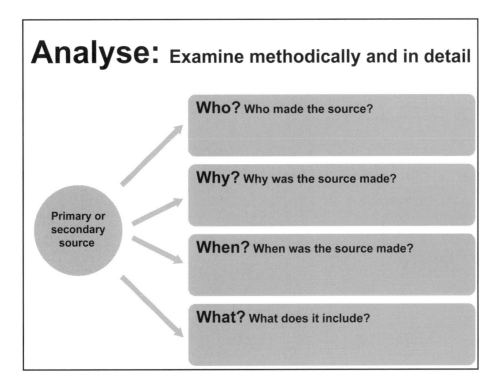

Worked example 2: slightly less support

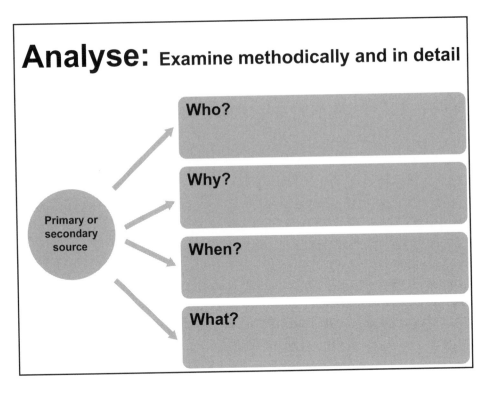

Worked example 3: even less support

In the final example, we're effectively back to the visual prompt we started with.

This might seem like a lot of work given the amount of content we have to cover, but focusing on skills can make our lives a lot easier thanks to their ability to cross over subject boundaries. For example, the ability to analyse isn't just useful in history; it's a skill we'd want to develop in other areas too, such as geography:

Learning (Key Stage 1)	● **Analyse** different sources of information to identify human and physical features.

If this was translated into a worked example (high scaffolding version), it might look like this:

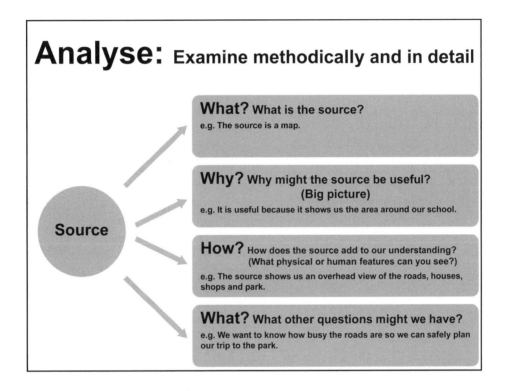

In terms of layout, it's identical to the one we used to analyse in history. There are some unavoidable changes to the words we've used because there will always be slight differences in the way the skill is applied in different subjects. In the big scheme of things, though, this doesn't really matter, and it's also not the end of the world if the children don't remember the exact combinations of 'what', 'why' or 'how' (although with enough repetition across the school there's a very good chance they will). What the children will learn is that being able to analyse something is an important and transferable skill, and thanks to the consistency of the definition and the strong visual prompt, they will have a clear idea of how to do it properly.

When they are able to look at a map (or whatever source you are interested in), identify what it is and give some information about why it would be useful, then we can start to get them thinking about how it might add to their knowledge and understanding by focusing on the physical and human features they can see.

We can go through exactly the same process for design technology:

Learning (Key Stage 2)	● Investigate and **analyse** examples of existing products.

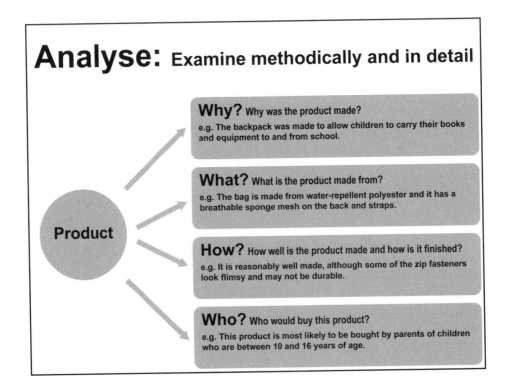

Or art:

Learning (Art and design – Key Stage 1)	**Analyse** works of art as a starting point for their own work.

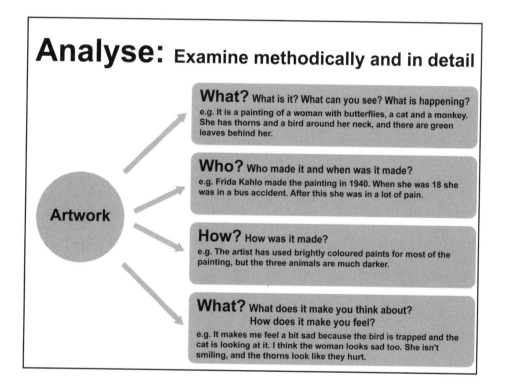

(Based on the painting *Self-Portrait with Thorn Necklace and Hummingbird* by Frida Kahlo, 1940)

The use of worked examples like this gives us a consistent approach to developing skills across the school, and it's not an approach that should be reserved for older children. It's not mastery if you only ever get to deepen your thinking when you're in Year 5 or Year 6. However, this doesn't mean they have to be used in exactly the same way.

If we consider the two examples from Key Stage 1 (for geography and art), the complexity and some of the detail in the examples in each box has been reduced, but there's still a lot in there if viewed as a whole. With younger children, there's no need to consider all of the aspects of 'analyse' in one go; we'd be much better off breaking it down to make it more manageable. If we were thinking about Year 1, then it might be that the only thing we focus on to start with in art would be the 'what'. We could model it once, and then have the children use a slimmed down version of the worked example to support them with this first stage:

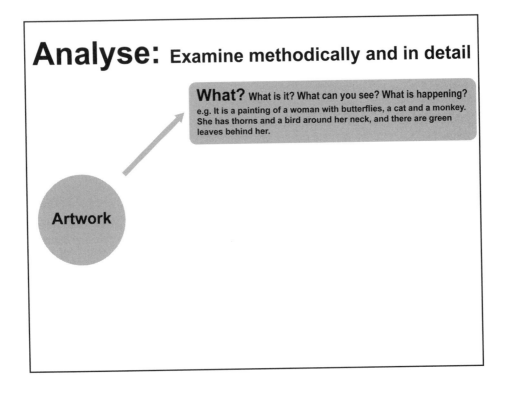

In the geography example, before getting on to how a source might add to our understanding, we might start with the 'what' and the 'why':

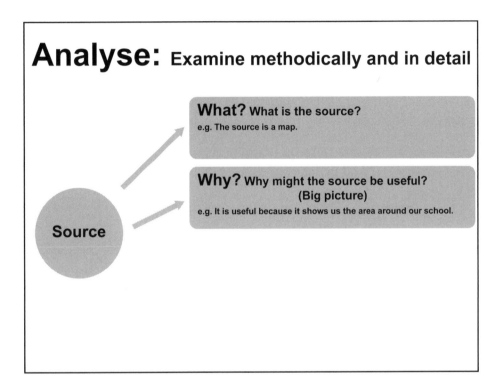

In both cases, the structure has stayed the same visually – we've just removed some information. This is important because we want the children to recognise the model when it's revisited later on in school and the blank space is eventually filled in with the other aspects of analysis. The definition, 'Examine methodically and in detail' has remained the same. I don't think there's any real benefit in changing this – we'd explain it to very young children by saying that it means 'look really closely', but I'm not a fan of shying away from using technical language. In fact, young children love difficult words and they seem to soak it up very easily. We start as we mean to go on.

There are a number of different options for how the children could use the worked examples. One option would be to write in the responses themselves.

They could do this independently or they could note down their thoughts on sticky notes which are added to a whole-class piece of work. If having the children write their own responses presents too much of a barrier, another option would be to have them scribed by an adult.

Ultimately, we're in no rush to develop the skill of analysing. If the children in Year 1 only get to the stage of learning how to identify the 'what', or the 'what' and the 'why', then they've got the rest of their time in school to develop their ability to analyse further, but what they've done is to make a great start. Regardless of how we adapt the worked examples, the most important thing is that we know what 'analyse', 'interpret', 'generalise', or any other skill for that matter, looks like. And if we're clear about this, then we've got something that we can apply to any area of the curriculum we like.

Deciding on a skills-based approach to the curriculum is easy, but actually making it happen in the classroom is the tricky bit. You can't develop this kind of stuff if you're trying to squeeze in everything. If you've only got six weeks to fit in your history, you'll be able to cover primary and secondary sources, but you'd be hard pushed to give the children the opportunity to learn how to interpret, analyse or generalise. Doing things properly takes time, but that's the price you pay for deeper learning.

Chapter 14

THE AWKWARD BANANA

Developing the practice of layered support and the introduction of self-selection had a massive impact on our children in terms of learning, but it's also had some repercussions that we weren't expecting, to do with the way our classrooms operate.

Before exploring this, it's worth taking a minute to consider why most primary classrooms around the country look pretty similar. When I was at primary school, I can remember sitting in semi-structured rows. We had one desk between two and there was a space between each desk on either side so the teacher had room to move around the tables. I was usually sitting next to a girl, which was likely to be the result of some early form of seating plan designed specifically to prevent me being with people I felt comfortable with (or, more likely, to stop me being naughty).

In other classes, the tables were pushed together to form groups. From memory, these seemed to be fairly mixed. I wasn't that good at maths, but it was alright because I sat next to Peter who was brilliant and let me copy. In both cases, the tables, whether individual or grouped, all faced the teacher's desk (and the blackboard) at the front.

When things got more prescriptive in terms of how teachers should teach, group work became more fashionable, and most classrooms around the country adopted the more modern set-up of pupils grouped around tables. Now, the term 'group work' was actually a little misleading as in most cases the pupils didn't really work as a group – they just sat together. What groups were actually for was to help with differentiation. We looked at differentiation from a learning perspective in Chapter 11, but the adoption of this as our default planning and teaching technique also had an impact on how we organised our classrooms. All of a sudden, we needed ability tables, and so it made perfect sense to arrange the furniture into groups of five. (Usually, in a class of thirty children, you'd get six around a table – five tables meant one lower ability, one higher ability and three middle-ish ones.)

Once you'd arranged your five or so tables, still mainly facing the front, there wasn't that much room left in the classroom, as there was also the stuff around the outside – drawer units, bookcases and the almost standard sink area.

With the layout of the classroom sorted, we then had to think about what to do with the resources. Primary school children need a lot of materials to do the things we want them to do. In any given lesson, they will need a pencil (or a pen for the special ones who have a pen licence[1]), a ruler (for underlining important things), mini-whiteboards, whiteboard pens and whiteboard rubbers, coloured pencils (but never for maths – apparently you have to crosshatch with a writing pencil – there is no place for colour in a maths book[2]) and felt tips (for special occasions). All of this has to go somewhere, but with space at a premium we haven't got many options.

After my first experience of Year 6 (juvenile delinquent class), I'd quickly learnt that the very best way to do this was to make sure that everything they needed was within easy reach in the middle of their tables. The main reason for this wasn't that they weren't physically capable of getting resources for themselves, it was more about what was likely to happen on the way. To get to the stuff they needed, they had to move past other tables, and because of the crampedness, this meant actually moving within flicking, elbowing and/or accidental nudging distance of other children. With pupils who had relatively short fuses, this was potentially explosive, and collecting a pencil could soon escalate into full-on fighting.

If they didn't need to move, there would be less fuss, and I could get on with the things that needed to be done. This desire to minimise fuss is evident in other classroom management techniques that we've evolved over time. Beyond just having the pens and pencils handy, there would be plenty of lessons in which the sheets/books/tablets/laminated bits and bobs/multilink cubes were sitting neatly on the tables alongside the pencil pots. When we got to the bit in the lesson when they needed something to work on or with, again they could reach into the middle and it would be there waiting. Most teachers like order and are quite rightly fearful of chaos. It also ties into the messages we are given about outstandingness which we considered earlier; along with making us do odd things

---

1 I know these things are popular, but you don't need a licence for a pen – just give them a pen. Please.
2 Feedback from the maths police (subject leader) on a lesson where I'd made the fatal mistake of allowing the children to shade fractions of shapes in an 'unmathematical colour'.

with our teaching, it has a similar impact on our classroom management and organisation.

If we want to maintain pace and/or demonstrate that we're making every single second of a lesson count, then we need to minimise unnecessary movement because movement leads to fuss, and fuss is the enemy of progress.

If we're honest, we could all reel off examples of this kind of overbearing organisation or routine, but if you're struggling to think of one, just consider for a second the level of resourcing (and back-up resourcing) that goes into lessons when we're being observed (particularly by inspectors). Suddenly, instead of the children having the standard six whiteboard pens on their table, they've now got twelve. They won't need them all – it's just in case – because the worst thing in the world would be for a child to not have what they need and as a result have to get up and move across the classroom to fetch it.

Sometimes routines stem from school-wide systems that have been in place for so long that no one has thought to ask why it exists or question whether it's actually doing any good. One school that I've visited even had routines for walking. Class 2 would begin by sitting on the carpet. The children were called in turn to join the line for the journey to assembly (via a well-established numbering system). When they reached the line, they had to place their right hand on the right shoulder of the child in front and keep it there until the whole class had lined up. When the instruction 'Arms!' was given by the teacher, the children silently took their hand off the child in front and folded their arms (creating uniform spacing between everyone in the line). They then began to move the short distance from classroom to school hall, punctuated every few seconds by the following commentary:

'That's excellent walking, Class 2.'

'I really like the way you're walking this morning, Ashley.'

'Look at you, Ahmed – arms folded, beautiful walking.'

'Oh Class 2 – this the best walking I've ever seen!'

By the time the teacher reached the hall she was exhausted, and when I asked her about it she said that she couldn't explain why it happened, just that 'it's what we've always done'.

My own personal example of ridiculousness can be found in the systems I created for the notoriously difficult business of snack time in Year 6. This happened after playtime because this is when it always happened. The children would come in from playtime, I'd read a story and they'd eat a snack. For this to run smoothly there were several meticulous steps that needed to be adhered to. First of all, I'd meet them at the steps outside my classroom where they'd be waiting at the bottom in some semblance of a line. I'd give my first instruction: 'OK children, when we go in, we're going to have a snack while I read the story. If you've got a snack in your bag, remember to bring it into class, then if you need milk, go and get it from next to the sink so you're ready at your table.' I'd then move a few feet from the top of the steps to the door and basically repeat the same instruction again – just in case.

Whilst the pupils were in the cloakroom, I'd pick off a few of the usual suspects for another reminder (the ones who never remembered to bring their snack in with them, despite the outstandingly clear instructions). After dealing with the cloakroom reprobates, I'd head to the front of the classroom and begin to direct proceedings from there: 'Well done, Amy – have you got your snack? Brilliant – don't forget your milk. Make sure you've got a straw ...' This went on until everyone was sitting down at their table, fruit and milk positioned in front of them, poised and waiting for me to start reading the story.

On most days, I'd get a sentence or two in before someone would stand up and attempt to put some form of fruit-related rubbish in the bin. I'd put a stop to this immediately and patiently remind them of the fact that we all put our rubbish away together, after we've finished. After a suitably long period of reading (largely determined by the size of the fruit they had to get through) we did exactly that: 'OK children, we're going to put our rubbish away now. Remember, fruit peel in the bin and milk cartons in the black sack – let's have Terrific table first ...'

After repeating this for each table in turn (with only six children moving around at any one time to keep things nice and calm), we were finally ready to get on with some learning. As routines go, it was foolproof, but as with the 'good walking' scenario, it was also really tiring. And because I'd set my stall out, it had to be the same every day – that was the point of routines. At the time, it was just how I managed my classroom. I wanted everything to run smoothly and believed that to achieve this, I needed systems and routines that managed every last detail.

My moment of realisation came in the form of one of the most incredible statements that I think I've heard as a teacher. It was an ordinary day and we were running through my special snack-time routine as normal. By this point I'd fine-tuned it all – the fruit-related reminders had been dished out and they were all sitting ready to listen to the class story whilst tucking into their fruit.

Someone would usually try to get up and move around as I started to read, but this wasn't the case today. Instead, after a paragraph or two, I noticed a hand being put up. It was coming from my 'higher ability' table (we were still in the dark old days of differentiation). I ignored it for a while, until it got more insistent and started waving at me.

It was Josh.[3] Now, Josh was well deserving of his place at the top table. He was brilliant at most things but particularly maths; even from the start of the year he was pretty much nailed on for a Level 6. (From the time when levels existed, as opposed to now when they still exist but we pretend they don't because we call them something different. Don't get me started …)

Anyway, if Josh needed something, it was obviously important. This is how the conversation went:

'What do you need, Josh?'

'Mr Lear, I can't do my banana.'

'What do you mean?'

'I mean it won't come out.'

End of conversation. Stunned silence.

Now, we talk a lot about children being secondary ready, but hand on heart, I think that if we send them up without the ability to successfully operate a banana then we're failing them.

Academically, Josh was probably in the top 5–10% nationally, but he was floored by the relatively straightforward task of opening an ever so slightly awkward banana. People like this exist in life – those who are academically brilliant but have no common sense. My initial thought was that maybe Josh was just one of

---

3 Name changed to prevent him being picked on by his friends.

these people. But the more I thought about it, the more examples I remembered of other occasions where the oldest and supposedly most capable children in the building had needed unusually high levels of support – the times when they sat with their hands up because they couldn't find a pencil in their pencil pot or they had reached the bottom of the page in their books and weren't sure what to do next.

It had been over ten years since I'd been a Year 1 teacher, but I had a sneaking feeling that this state of affairs hadn't always been the case. To double check, I decided to go and spend some time with our youngest children in the Early Years, just for a comparison. The first thing that hit me was the organisation of snack time. They had a table for snacks. It had a sign on it that said 'Snacks', and the fruit was sitting on the table in a basket. When the children wanted to have their snack, they temporarily stopped the thing they were doing, went to the snack table, had their snack (possibly whilst having a chat to anyone else on the table who was doing the same thing) before depositing any rubbish in the bin and going back to whatever it was they were doing before.

There was absolutely no adult involvement at all – not even someone to praise them for the quality of their walking. I'm not suggesting there had never been any adult involvement, but thanks to whatever modelling had gone on earlier, I was witnessing reception age children who were operating at a level way beyond my class of Year 6s.

Beyond snacks, they also seemed to have the almost magical ability to get resources for themselves, and then, even more miraculously, put them back where they belonged (without having to be told seventeen times). There seemed to be so much freedom but without any sense of chaos. It was like the teachers had ignored the fact that the children were only four years old and given them the kind of responsibility that's not usually seen until you hit university.

I went back to Year 6 with my head buzzing and decided that the very best thing I could do with my classroom was to make it resemble the Early Years as closely as was humanly possible. My first attempt was with snacks. To start with, I cleared some space on top of one of the drawer units at the side of the classroom and made myself a fancy sign that said 'Snacks'. I then found five small baskets so that each table could keep their fruit together and hopefully reduce the chances of them accidentally eating someone else's satsuma.

With the practicalities sorted, I spoke to the children about it and explained what I'd seen in reception. They were definitely interested and believed themselves capable of operating with the same independence as their younger colleagues, so with everyone on the same page, we gave it a go.

Day one was a complete disaster. Lots of them forgot to put their fruit in the baskets in the first place, and for those who did, they seemed to deliberately pick the worst possible moment to go and get it. I'd be regaling them with some fascinating teaching point about non-defining relative clauses and mid-flow they'd get up and wander over to the fruit baskets.

There's a critical point here: my old system worked; the new one apparently didn't. But just because something works, it doesn't necessarily make it desirable. And just because something doesn't work the first time we try it, it doesn't mean it has no merit. I decided that we needed some time, and that expecting success on day one was a bit ridiculous given the fact that the children had experienced six years of independence-sapping spoon-feeding.

Day two was a little bit better after we decided on a rule: no one was allowed to go to the fruit baskets when I was teaching but they could go at any other point. They were happy with that and it worked. Over time (and we're talking weeks here), more and more of them remembered to put their fruit in the baskets and they started to make sensible decisions about when to go and collect it. If there were a couple of people over there waiting, then they'd sit tight for a while. What they loved the most was the freedom to decide when to go for themselves. Some of them even devised their own system depending on which fruit they'd brought in and the particular lesson they were doing. One girl told me that if she'd brought in an apple, she'd always eat it during English, but if it was grapes, that was definitely a more mathsy fruit. Some other less imaginative children just went when they were hungry.

The success of this, and the fact that the children thought it was the best thing ever, made me think about the other aspects of our day-to-day classroom life that could be rethought in a similar way. The fetching and replacing of resources was a big thing, and something I desperately wanted to do differently. Because of the issues described earlier, I still wasn't comfortable with having the children moving around the classroom to collect what they needed, but this was based on the idea that they'd all be heading to a single place.

Even in classrooms with pencil pots and resources on every table, there's still usually an additional central resource area where spare stuff (and the class pencil sharpener) is kept. They're generally not well used and can often seem invisible because the children never think to go there when they can't find what they're looking for. (Although, it's more likely that they don't head there because if they're found to be out of their seat without permission then they know they'll get it in the neck.)

The idea of having a central resource area would be alien to most talented Early Years teachers. They would have worked out within moments that creating a single point that all children have to access is a no-no. A bottle neck of four-year-olds is no more desirable than the equivalent with Year 6s. Instead, they organise things differently, and for ease of access have multiple points around the room where the most useful resources are clustered – the children simply have to go to the nearest available station.

The realisation that the children didn't need to move that far for me to encourage their independence was a useful one. After all, if you have to decide what it is you need, then go and collect it before using it and putting it back; it doesn't matter whether you've travelled two steps or twenty – you still had to do it for yourself.

This meant that one of the easiest shifts I made was to move things from the middle of the tables to a place quite close by. It wasn't within arm's reach but it wasn't on the other side of the classroom – a happy compromise. Again, the change wasn't without its teething problems, but we kept at it and before long the children had got used to their new-found responsibility and had rediscovered some of their long-lost independence.

This kind of small-scale experimentation is really important and comes directly from pausing to ask questions about existing practice. I'm not 100% sold on the idea of teachers as researchers – at least, not in any formal or scientific sense. I love a bit of research, but as things stand, it's difficult to see how we'd have the time to be playing around with randomised controlled trials or other fancy methodologies. What I am interested in, though, is trying things out – to pinch the words of Zora Neale Hurston, 'poking and prying with a purpose'[4] – and in some cases, the smallest bit of experimentation can lead to significant changes in the way we view our practice.

---

4 Z. N. Hurston, *Dust Tracks on a Road: An Autobiography* (London: Hutchinson & Co., 1942), p. 91.

Chapter 15

CAVEMAN DAVE AND THE TARDIS

One of my more useful personality traits/disorders is a fairly constant restlessness. The small-scale shifts in practice that we've just looked at should perhaps have been enough, but there was a nagging thought that even though things were better, there was definitely more that could be done – not just in terms of the children's general independence but also to support their learning.

Before getting into this, there's some thinking to be done in terms of what it is we actually want from a classroom. For me, this can be boiled down to a set of key aims that sum up (in no particular order) what I'm after:

- A place that children are desperate to come to.
- A place that teachers are desperate to come to (or, on a bad day, at least slightly inclined).
- A place that supports a mastery approach to the curriculum.
- A place that supports independence.

This isn't supposed to be a definitive list of what a classroom has to do, and there are certainly things missing (i.e. a place with a decent cupboard to hide the stuff that I don't want anyone else to see), but as guiding aims, they're not a bad place to start.

The first two points aren't really anything to do with learning; they're possibly more important than that. Beyond the absolutely essential non-negotiables of classrooms being safe, secure, accessible and welcoming, creating the kind of environment that functions like a massive magnet can have a huge impact on what young people think and feel about their time in school.

As a Year 1 teacher, I always believed that making my classroom appealing and stimulating was just part and parcel of the job. Fortunately, I had quite a lot of help from our long-suffering building supervisor, Andy, who whilst doing many other things around school, could also knock up a pretty impressive-looking display in next to no time. One of our favourite creations was a 'cave' in the corner of the classroom. It started with us just covering an underused reading/group work area with sheets of grey sugar paper, but it quickly snowballed into not just the entrance to a cave but the dwelling place of Caveman Dave.[1] Before I knew it, Andy had been at the MDF and a four-foot replica of Dave appeared outside the cave, complete with faux fur animal skin outfit. After this, things got slightly out of hand, and Dave was quickly followed by a fully working (albeit historically questionable) caveman car.

The point of it all was to create awe and wonder, and it definitely had the effect we were after. The children thought it was amazing, and were desperate to be in it, near it or around it for as much of the time as possible.

After the move to Year 6, I was more tentative. I had nice-looking displays, but I didn't risk the larger scale immersive stuff – at least, not to begin with. It took me considerably longer than it should have done to realise that Year 6s are still children. I think I'd convinced myself that they were mini-adults who didn't need all of the trappings that we normally associate with Key Stage 1. It turned out I was wrong.

One of the first things I had a go at was the reading area. To call it a 'reading area' is slightly misleading. It was just a tall bookcase with books on it. The 'area' part of its name was also redundant because the children did all their reading back at their tables. My first thought was just to jazz it up a little. At the time, the children were really into *Doctor Who*, which had just started up again on the telly. Taking advantage of this piece of knowledge, I decided to dress up the book shelf as the TARDIS. I think I might have also come up with a catchy slogan for the wall – probably something incredibly creative like 'Travel into a black hole of books!' For added authenticity, the bookshelf was topped off with a blue flashing light, mainly to flag up to the less observant children that something was different.

I was hoping for a few positive comments from the children, but was also braced for the cynicism that I'd assumed was a prerequisite of being eleven. The actual response from the children surprised me. They appeared to be as excited as the Year 1s had been over the cave. They genuinely seemed to think it was incredible. This led to further developments. We got a rug and some space-themed cushions to sit on, and then the final piece of the jigsaw fell into place with the addition of a couple of king-size black bed sheets (available at a knockdown price on

---

1   Dave won't (or shouldn't) need any introduction to fellow Year 1 teachers as he features in the eponymously titled *Caveman Dave* by the brilliant Nick Sharratt (London: Walker Books, 2007).

account of the fact that it wasn't the 1980s any more). The sheets were pinned to the wall and ceiling to create a canopy and finished off with some sparkly stars and masses of glitter.

Suddenly, this became an area that the children would kill to spend some time in. They insisted that we did all sorts of whole-class stuff under the canopy – I'd read to them or whatever else it was, and they'd quite happily tolerate the ridiculously cramped conditions, just like the Year 1s who'd forced me to teach maths in Dave's under-proportioned cave.

The difference it made to the children was amazing, and this was just one little area of the classroom. It's not uncommon to find classrooms with similarly engaging reading areas, although this is still more common in Key Stage 1 than in Key Stage 2. I decided to take things further. What if it wasn't just one area? What if the theme spread out across the whole classroom?

I chose a space theme because of the *Doctor Who* connection, but given the nature of the projects we've looked at, there are plenty of ready-made themes that could tie in directly to the children's learning. If we think about an enquiry question such as, 'How do we make our mark?' from which the children might explore concepts such as 'protest', 'class', 'power', 'influence' and 'democracy', then we could start by creating a speakers' corner in the classroom by strapping together some old milk crates. This theme could be continued with banners hung from the ceiling adorned with slogans and quotes, or maybe a series of large placards could be used to display the question.

In this instance, the immersive theme links directly to the concepts that will be explored, but it can also be developed from either the curriculum content or the outcome of a project. In the Year 2 example in Chapter 5, the question was, 'Do we always appreciate what we've got?' and the curriculum focus was the rainforest. The most obvious way to create an immersive environment for this project would be to go for a rainforest effect. A few washing lines crisscrossing the room draped with some fake ivy or crepe paper vines and you've cracked it. Add in the potted fern you've acquired from the head's office and the inflatable parrot from the end-of-term do and you might as well be in the Amazon.

In a Year 3 arts-themed project, it was the outcome that decided the theme. Concepts of 'happiness', 'individuality', 'identity' and 'creativity' were explored through the enquiry question, 'Is it better to stand out or fit in?' As part of the project, the children were tasked with designing a costume that represented, reflected and celebrated their own personality. The emphasis here was on design rather than actually making a full costume, and the children worked with a professional costume department from the Crucible Theatre in Sheffield to create mood boards. The theme in this case linked directly to the outcome, so the classroom became a designers' studio, with fabric draped from the washing lines, costumes hung from clothes rails and a couple of dressmaker's dummies dotted around the room for added effect.

Getting the balance right is important – we don't want to go so full on that it's distracting, but with some careful thought, a quick search on the internet for some inspiration and a little bit of effort, we can create spaces that move children from just learning about something to actually living and breathing it.

There is always an immersive theme to be developed – it can start small, but why restrict your creativity to a display board or a corner of the room when the classroom is your oyster?[2] Investing in the classroom environment in this way also has the welcome knock-on effect of making it a place that we want to be in just as much as the children. It's partly because of the sense of pride you get from the effort you've made, but mostly it's because of the look on the children's faces when they come through the classroom door.

2 If you happen to be a school leader or head teacher reading this and you find yourself nodding along, then how about carving out some time for teachers to do it properly? What difference would it make to the quality of the environment if a teacher had a whole day without the children in the classroom to get it done?

Chapter 16

MASTERY AND INDEPENDENCE

If we return to the idea of layering support, it's clear that we've got a powerful means of building independence within the learning process, but it's difficult to scatter your nuts effectively if you don't have a clearing in which to do it.

First of all, using a layered support approach alongside self-selection is definitely doable with a traditional classroom set-up. For this to work, though, we have to accept that there's going to be more fluidity than we've been used to previously. If the children still have their own place (mixed ability but with a seating plan), then you'll need to have the full range of support on every table so they can genuinely self-select.

If this works well, then happy days, but there's also the risk that old habits will resurface. Maybe we try to save on the printing or we only have one box of Numicon,[1] and we end up placing certain things on certain tables. The highly scaffolded worked examples make it onto the tables where most of the middle ability children sit, the Numicon heads straight to the lower ability lot, and before we know it we're back to square one.

If we scatter the different forms of layered support around the room and allow the children to select what they need before finding their way back to their table, then we've got to be comfortable with them moving around. If this is worked on, it can be really effective: the children are not just taking control of the support they need for their learning, they're also managing and organising their own resources (thanks to the clustering we looked at in Chapter 13). If it's not worked on, however, then we'll find ourselves 'managing' the process for them, and again our good intentions are undermined.

There's a bit of the square peg in a round hole thing going on here. We've got a much more flexible understanding of how to approach learning, but we're still trying to squeeze it into a classroom that was designed for a much more rigid

---

1   If you've never come across Numicon, or you haven't got a decent amount in school, then speak to your maths subject leader and persuade them to get their hands on some. Along with good old Dienes blocks and Cuisenaire rods, they're one of the most useful manipulatives you can have in the classroom. (They also come in a range of thoroughly unmathematical colours.)

approach. If we're interested in taking full advantage of layered support and self-selection, then we need to go back to the idea we examined in Chapter 5 of adapting rather than adopting.

The first thing to consider is whether we actually need all of the stuff that's currently in our classroom. In the Early Years, classrooms operate with a much less formal structure, and it would be unusual to find the rooms cluttered with enough tables and chairs for every child to sit at them simultaneously. I'd always assumed that bigger children were different. In some schools, the point at which children are ready for a formal classroom layout is when they hit Year 1 – aged five. I'm not sure what the thinking behind this is: maybe something happens to a five-year-old that means the very best way to educate them is to have them sitting at a table for five hours a day, but I'm not convinced. As a matter of fact, I'm not convinced that it's effective for eleven-year-olds either.

As a teacher, I bought into it – I felt I didn't have much of a choice. When I first started as an NQT in Year 1, I inherited a classroom full of tables and just got on with it. When I moved to Year 6, the classroom was almost identical, just with bigger chairs. I only really stopped to think about it when I started to notice what happened when the children were given a choice.

This was something I noticed first at home. One Christmas, Imogen and Eve got given some little wooden desks with chairs. They were the type that have a flip-up lid to keep your bits and bobs in and were delivered in the hope that they might somehow contain the spread of pens/pencils/glitter that enveloped the house. After the Christmas Day excitement that comes from unwrapping a desk, they were placed side by side in the girls' room and we sat back and waited for the obvious benefits to kick in. It never happened. Neither of them even came close to sitting and working at the desks. They stored bits and pieces in there, but when they were working/playing/being busy, they did what they'd always done and spread out everywhere else. Imogen would be deep in concentration with a sticker book whilst laid out full length on the floor. Eve could be found on the sofa, surrounded by sheets of writing or drawings. It was almost as if they were deliberately trying to punish Father Christmas for bringing them such an unimaginative gift. Or maybe they were just more comfortable working in a different space.

I then started to notice the same phenomenon in school. The *Doctor Who* theme that I'd set up in Year 6 started life as a reading area, but before long it became a place where the children wanted to do their writing, maths or art work. Obviously, they couldn't all use it, so it became a reward – if the children worked hard (or bought me a bag of my favourite sweets), I'd let them work in there for a while, spread out on the rugs and cushions.

Even as an adult, I don't always choose to sit and work at a table. Right now, I am. I've got stuff everywhere – papers, notes, a pile of books and a cup of tea. I like being able to spread out. If I'm doing something on my laptop, like checking emails, then I'm happier on the sofa. As a Year 6 teacher, I'd inevitably have the odd SATs practice test to mark, so to speed things up I sit on the floor and mark the same question in six or so papers at the same time with them all laid out around me. I suppose it depends on the job in hand, but I'm a grown-up so I get to decide for myself.

If we've facilitated self-selection of support, then what about some self-selection in terms of *how* and *where* the children work? One way of achieving this is to ditch some of the existing tables and chairs and think about adapting the room to include a range of different working areas. When we first experimented with this at school, we started tentatively. A couple of tables went and were replaced with some big floor cushions. The children loved it. After a week or so, the teachers were pushing more and more tables out of the room to create even more space. All of a sudden, the classrooms didn't feel cramped and crowded – there was space to move. Layers of support and other resources could now be easily accessed and the layout of the room could be adapted and changed to fit the learning that was happening.

Some of the tables were replaced with low level versions that didn't require chairs (cheap and cheerful coffee tables with the legs chopped down), and we got hold of some A3 clipboards that meant the children always had a surface to rest on (or clip their book onto), regardless of where they chose to sit.

Over time, as we saw more and more evidence of this working, we kept at it. In Year 5 and 6, we added tall cafe-style tables and stools (to create a range of heights in the room), some stepped seating areas covered in fake grass and a sofa or two. All of the changes were about how the room functioned rather than how it looked, and came from us watching and noticing how the children operated. We observed the kinds of areas they chose to work in, whether they had different preferences depending on what they were doing, and what it was they seemed to need in order to be comfortable.

As well as thinking about these things from the children's perspective, we also had our teacher heads on. We were understandably concerned that behaviour would suffer when we removed the structure of a formal classroom, but we actually found that the opposite was true. The classrooms became calmer, quieter and more purposeful places, even for some of our most challenging cohorts. Linked to the behaviour angle, we were also wary about the choices the children would make in terms of who they worked with and whether, if they always chose to sit with their friends, they would just be talking and wasting their time. Lots of the children did work alongside their friends (particularly in Key Stage 2 when they tend to get tribal), but our solution was to constantly repeat the same mantra: 'You need to choose someone to work with who will bring out your best.' If, for whatever reason, we felt that a child wasn't producing their best work or that their effort wasn't right, we would just remove the choice and tell them where to sit. This quickly became one of the worst things we could do to the children, which says a lot about how much they valued the choice.

Another thing we kept an eye on was the presentation of the children's work. Some people are quite keen on the idea that the only way to produce beautifully presented work or neat handwriting is by insisting on correct posture at a desk. We found that there was no deterioration at all in presentation – where it had been a bit dodgy, it was still a bit dodgy, and where it had been excellent, it was still excellent.[2]

Developing classrooms like this didn't create independent children overnight. The younger children in Key Stage 1 took to it far more quickly than those in Key Stage 2, perhaps because they weren't that far removed from the Early Years and remembered how it all worked. With the older classes, we spent time training (or retraining) them, and within the space of a term, they were about as autonomous as your average four-year-old.

The impact of adapting our classroom environments was huge, but I can't really back this up with anything other than what I've seen and the conversations I've had with teachers and children. There's no data to support this, and whilst the children's progress and attainment is great, we can't pin it on just one factor. The

---

2   There's something of an obsession with handwriting at the moment and, if I'm being honest, it winds me up. Because we use the critique process, we do a lot of redrafting. As far as I'm concerned, a draft is a work in progress and it just needs to be legible. It doesn't need to be written in perfect cursive handwriting. When we're working on the finished piece of work, that's when I expect it to be incredible.

classroom environment definitely helps, and the sense of responsibility and independence that the children developed ripples through everything they do.

Rethinking our classrooms in this way might sound risky, but there's nothing revolutionary about any of it. The changes we've made are rooted in Early Years practice; we're just taking an approach that works and looking at how it can be developed throughout the entire school. It's a model of good practice that we've been ignoring in education for far too long.

Chapter 17

THE MONKEY-PROOF BOX

The desire to learn from Early Years practice brings us neatly to the last aspect of a blended pedagogy: the monkey-proof box. Making life difficult might seem counterintuitive. It's not something we're usually concerned with, as life in school can be hard enough without deliberately going out of our way to stuff things up even more.

Having said that, there's definitely some mileage in embracing awkwardness, and by fine-tuning our direct teaching and developing our thinking about how we facilitate learning, we've created the perfect conditions to start thinking about how to add complexity and challenge.

We've started to think more carefully about the idea of introducing difficulty over the past couple of years – particularly in maths. For the majority of my career, we were stuck in a pattern of teaching place value in maths for the first two weeks in September. In fact, if you'd gone into any school in the country, you'd have found much the same thing going on because we were all following the same basic plan. After this, we'd move on to addition, multiplication or whatever else we were supposed to be doing. At the end of the two-week block, we were pretty pleased with ourselves because the children would have lots of work in their books which all seemed to be right. I really only noticed the problem after moving to Year 6, where I found that, despite having being taught place value throughout their time in school, many of the children didn't seem to have any kind of grasp of it at all.

One of the benefits of going for a mastery approach to maths has been a shift in this type of thinking. Two weeks on possibly the most fundamental part of maths was never enough, so to do it properly we now do it for longer. This ties into the idea of the difference between performance and learning that we looked at in Chapter 11. The children didn't learn place value in two weeks, they simply performed. Subconsciously, I think we probably knew this was the case, because we didn't go out of our way to test the strength of their learning; it was easier to believe that it had gone in and then move on.

As teachers, we've generally been trained to make the children's lives easier rather than harder, so deliberately trying to catch them out wouldn't necessarily be something that we're overly keen on. Now, if the children can complete a process procedurally, instead of moving them on to whatever comes next, we can try to assess how well they understand it. We can wrap this up as 'deepening', 'mastery' or 'challenge', but, essentially, what it boils down to is going out of our way to make things awkward. If we reframe the learning or ask the children to apply it in a different or unusual context, and they can do it, then this gives us the confidence to say that they have mastered it. Whether this approach has managed to seep out into other areas of the curriculum is debatable, but there's no reason why this thinking shouldn't apply to everything.

If children can write simple sentences, then instead of reaching for the pot of conjunctions and throwing in an 'and', we can push them into thinking harder about what they're already doing: 'Can you write a simple sentence that describes the setting using exactly nine words?' or 'Can you write a simple sentence that describes the setting without using any adjectives?' Automatically, the restriction means that as well as concentrating on the mechanics of constructing a simple sentence, they've now got an added element to think about. If their learning is shaky, they will struggle; if they've mastered it, then being forced into considering the words they're choosing more carefully might be a challenge, but it won't be a problem.

By accepting that modelling extends beyond our direct teaching, we've reduced the amount of time we need to spend front and centre and increased the time we've got for a different sort of interaction – talking to the children. In terms of actually making a difference to the process of learning, there isn't any better use of our time, and to make the most of this, there are some specific things we can do. One of the easiest is to ensure that the children are using the layers of support effectively. Ideally, this will involve some facilitation at most, because the aim of layering support is to have the children accessing it independently. Whilst we're at it, we'll also be asking questions to check for understanding and keeping an eye out for mistakes and errors.[1] When we get beyond this, things get more interesting.

The idea of feedback is often misunderstood, and we've been led to believe that it's a one-way street: teachers provide feedback to their pupils. It doesn't matter whether it's verbal, written or via the medium of contemporary dance, it's the teacher who supplies it. What this misses is the fact that the most valuable form of feedback happening in any lesson is (or at least should be) the feedback from the pupil to the teacher. This is when we notice misconceptions and misunderstandings. We then feed this into our understanding of where the children are currently in terms of the learning, where they need to go next and how this might happen.

This is how teachers in the Early Years operate, where the importance of noticing stuff (and sometimes obsessively writing it down on sticky notes) is standard and highly effective practice. Along with observing how the children are progressing with their learning, the other thing we're on the lookout for are those who appear to have got it all sorted. If a child's success is as a result of highly scaffolded support (via a worked example), then we can encourage them to adjust the level of challenge by switching to one of the faded examples so they've got less to go on. But if they are genuinely demonstrating that they've moved from performance to learning, then a different approach is needed.

We touched on the idea of restrictions in the context of simple sentences, but it's a very useful way to create awkwardness in other areas too. I've already mentioned the fact that we've made great inroads with maths, so the following example now feels like a fairly natural response to children who've learnt the thing we're interested in – in this case, area and perimeter: 'OK, so I know you understand area and perimeter, but can you create a shape with an area of 12cm^2 and a perimeter of 16cm or less?'

The restriction isn't complicated, but it means that instead of moving on, we've created some difficulty that edges the children towards thinking harder about the process they're going through. Beyond this, we could tinker with the restriction

---

1   We define 'mistakes' as being the things they've got wrong but shouldn't have – it might be a missed capital letter when they do know better or a forgotten ear on their portrait. Usually a quick finger point is enough to set things straight before moving on. An 'error', on the other hand, is something that stems from a misconception and will be addressed either by referring to a specific part of the worked example or by doing some remodelling for clarification.

a little more to give them another nudge: 'How many shapes could you create with an area of 12cm² and a perimeter that's equal to or greater than 22cm?'

If we think about the different aspects of creative thinking that we looked at in Part I, then this kind of increasing restriction is exactly what we need to draw it out: asking questions, exploring possibilities, overcoming barriers, adapting ideas, making connections – it's all there. And by applying the same thinking, we can create the same conditions for any area of the curriculum we like.

In PE, a restriction might work its magic by tweaking the rules: 'OK, for the next two minutes, you're only allowed two touches of the football before passing it.' In dance, it might be the challenge of creating a motif in which there's always two points of contact with the floor. In art, we might ask a child to complete a sketch without removing their pencil from the paper or restrict the tools or media from which they can select. In science, we could ask, 'Can you design an investigation using only a ball and a tape measure?' or 'Can you classify the materials using criteria other than size, shape or colour?' In design technology, 'Can you show me five different ways of joining the materials without using a glue stick or a stapler?' or 'Can you design a vehicle that moves without using wheels?'

In each case, the restriction is dropped in when there's a level of expertise to be tested. There's no point attempting to play a small-sided game of football using only two touches if the children can't control the ball or pass accurately, but when the timing is right, a restriction is the perfect way to disrupt what would otherwise be an unhelpfully smooth process.

After an initial restriction, further difficulties can be added in layers to increase the complexity. Maybe after limiting the number of touches of the football, we start to limit the space in which the game is played. After designing a vehicle that moves without using wheels, we might constrain the materials that are available for use.

Another approach to developing this kind of difficulty is the idea of wonderings. I briefly described these in my first book, *Guerrilla Teaching*, as they're a very useful way of not just adding a little awkwardness but also of encouraging a climate of curiosity. To get this right, the teacher needs to know exactly what they're talking about in terms of subject knowledge. Of course, this should be a given, but rather than sharing it with anyone who will listen, instead we need to pretend that we don't have it at all.

If we take the context of the children learning about triangles (and specifically internal angles), it might go like this:

In our heads …	'Good – you've worked out that the sum of the interior angles of an equilateral triangle is 180 degrees. Now I want to see if you can work out that this is a rule that applies to all triangles.'
	↓
Out loud …	'I wonder if it's always the case that the angles in a triangle add up to 180 degrees?'

And after that:

In our heads …	'OK, you've established a rule for triangles, but can you apply this thinking to other shapes?'
	↓
Out loud …	'I wonder what would happen if we tried it with quadrilaterals?'

And if we wanted to keep going:

In our heads …	'OK, you've got quadrilaterals sorted – let's see if you can spot a pattern in shapes with more than four sides.'
	↓
Out loud …	'I don't suppose there's a rule for polygons too – I wonder if you can find it?'

Again, timing is everything – a misplaced wondering can do more harm than good – but positioning ourselves as a curious simpleton isn't selling us short. It's purely about getting our children to do the thinking for themselves, and with it, develop the kind of curiosity that befits our small Amazonian sex-obsessed cousins.

Beyond looking at how these types of difficulties can be introduced as part of the learning process, it's also worth considering how the concept of desirable difficulties might make us think differently about the structure of learning. The term 'desirable difficulty' was coined by the cognitive psychologist Robert Bjork, who used the idea to explore the impact that awkwardness can have on learning – and, in particular, the retention of learning.[2] His work throws up some interesting ideas that have some very practical applications in four different areas: generation, spacing, interleaving and perceptual difficulties.

First, we'll have a look at the least useful of the four – perceptual difficulties. This focuses on the idea that making something more difficult to read (by using a weird font, blurring words or having very small print) leads to deeper processing and therefore better remembering. It's more technical than I've made it sound but that's the basic idea. Whether or not it actually makes a difference is debatable, but it does seem to go against my usual mode of operation. If I think

---

2   E. L. Bjork and R. A. Bjork, Making Things Hard on Yourself, but in a Good Way: Creating Desirable Difficulties to Enhance Learning. In M. A. Gernsbacher, R. W. Pew, L. M. Hough and J. R. Pomerantz (eds), *Psychology and the Real World: Essays Illustrating Fundamental Contributions to Society* (New York: Worth Publishers, 2011), pp. 56–64.

about how I used to differentiate for my lower ability (lemons group) children in a lesson that needed some key language, I'd always have it printed out and ready for them to use. In doing so, I'd also print the words in a nice large font because, as well as assuming they were a bit thick, I seemed to think that they couldn't see very well either. Maybe, instead of going out of my way to make the text easy to access, I should have been doing the opposite – or at least I should have thought more deeply about what I was up to.

Although I'm in no great rush to change all my fonts, the three other areas that Bjork investigated deserve more attention. The idea of generation works on the premise that there are greater long-term benefits from generating words, answers or processes ourselves, rather than just being given them. It's got to be better to remember stuff for yourself than having it offered up on a plate, but whether or not we've had this realisation, there's little evidence of it having had any impact on the way in which most of us have been encouraged to structure our lessons. For as long as I can remember, it's been considered good practice amongst most teachers to start a new lesson with a recap. The 'recap prior learning' bit has survived various shifts in the evolution of our lesson structure, but maybe it's time for us to think about it differently. If we're honest, in any given lesson, most of the recap is actually being done by the teacher. We do the remembering, whether it's by repeating language or referring to an image or process from the day before on an interactive whiteboard. It doesn't really make sense when you think about it. Making life too easy – or, more specifically, making recall too easy – is doing away with a vital part of the whole learning process. If the children aren't given the opportunity to remember for themselves, then there's a good chance they won't remember anything at all.

So, if we're not starting lessons with a recap, how do we start them? It's difficult to answer this without rephrasing the question. First of all, we shouldn't be bothering with lessons per se. If learning only happens over time, then the idea of a lesson automatically becomes less important. We're not expecting anything miraculous to happen in our sixty-minute window of opportunity, so we can stop worrying about it and start creating the conditions for learning instead.

If we consider the shift from learning to performance, and how we can use layers of support to manage it, then we're already thinking the right thoughts. At the start of the learning process, it's likely that there will be direct teaching. This modelling is then continued through the layered support so the children can practise and be successful (performance). After this supported practice, and having spent time talking about/listening to/generally noticing what the children are up to, it may well be the end of the session. If this takes an hour, then it's taken an hour – not because that's the length of the slot on the timetable, but because at around sixty minutes, it felt like the right time to stop. If it takes less time, then this is OK – it's only the start of the process. If it takes longer because we've built in a break or paused for a banana, then this is good too.

No matter how long it takes, it's got to stop at some point (we've all got homes to go to), and this leaves us with the problem of how to start things up again. Traditionally, lesson two would begin with the aforementioned recap and then some teaching. What we're interested in now, though, is not the next lesson but the next stage in the learning. This changes our priorities, and if we take on board the advice around generation, then we're better off structuring things so the hard work is done by the children. For the second session we might actually stick with the idea of a recap, but instead of it being about the learning, it would focus on the layer of support that the children had used to be successful: 'OK, yesterday we made a great start with our learning about … [insert whatever it is]. I want you to think about what resources you used to be successful, and what you're aiming to use today.'

Now, this will only work if the children understand the point of weaning themselves off the layers of support (and are motivated enough to want to do so), but given the fact that we've been drip-feeding the concept of a 'great start' into their daily diet, they should respond in exactly the way we want. Following this, we can get straight back into a period of deliberate practice, with the children primed to reflect on the stage they're up to in their learning and also to consider the best way to move forwards.[3]

To help with this process, one of the things we can do is to display an overview of the learning that sets out the different stages and/or layers of support that are being used along the way. This can be as simple as pinning up a sheet of paper showing arrows linking the stages. At a glance, the children can see their learning mapped out and use it to help them decide what they're going to do next.

---

3 This process is exactly what we mean by 'metacognition' (the ways in which learners monitor and direct their learning). If you're interested in seeing some of the research that backs up this thinking, there's a very useful guidance report by the Education Endowment Foundation called *Metacognition and Self-Regulated Learning* (London: EEF, 2018). Available at: https://educationendowmentfoundation.org.uk/evidence-summaries/teaching-learning-toolkit/meta-cognition-and-self-regulation.

Timing wise, if we're removing the necessity to go through the whole teaching process again, then we also need to get rid of the need for it to take an hour. It might be that this second session takes twenty minutes, but it will be twenty minutes of deliberate practice. In a traditional lesson the children would only get this much practice time anyway, after taking into account all of the recapping, remodelling, instructing and mini-plenaries thrown into the mix.

This approach should make us think much more flexibly about our timetables; learning doesn't fit into neat hour-long chunks, so we shouldn't try to force it. If we're clear about how learning works, then it follows that we should be the ones to decide how to map it out.

Finally, we come to spacing and interleaving. The idea of using spaced intervals between learning (and ideas about its impact) has been around for quite a while. However, this isn't something that most schools have paid too much attention to, largely because of its apparent incompatibility with the 'rapid and sustained' progress bandwagon which saw us rattle off sequences of sixty-minute lessons before moving on to a new topic. With a better understanding of long-term learning, as opposed to short-term (and short-lived) gains, it's something we might start to think about more seriously.

At its simplest, spacing means that we're leaving gaps between each 'reloading' of the learning and, as a result, creating the conditions in which the children have to work harder at remembering. If we take English and maths as an example, the traditional model has been to deliver five literacy and five numeracy lessons a week – usually organised into hour-long slots in the timetable (example 1).

Monday	Maths session 1	English session 1			
Tuesday	Maths session 2	English session 2			
Wednesday	Maths session 3	English session 3			
Thursday	Maths session 4	English session 4			
Friday	Maths session 5	English session 5			

Example 1

Whilst this might vary a little – maybe it's English first, then maths, or maybe it alternates between the two across the week – it's fairly common practice in most schools, and you could even argue that this set-up is compatible with the idea of spacing. After beginning the learning in maths session 1 on Monday, we switch to English, and then whatever else we fill up the empty slots with, before returning to maths and 'reloading' the learning on Tuesday morning in maths session 2. There's no doubt about the fact that there's a space between the first two maths sessions, but this pattern doesn't make much of an effort to optimise the effect. Above all, if we accept that we don't need to be bound by the hour-long lesson rule, then we can adopt a more flexible approach and increase the number of times the learning can be reloaded by the children.

Monday		Maths session 1 (45 mins)		
Tuesday	Maths session 2 (20 mins)		Maths session 3 (20 mins)		
Wednesday			Maths session 4 (25 mins)		Maths session 5 (20 mins)
Thursday		Maths session 6 (25 mins)		Maths session 7 (20 mins)	
Friday					Maths session 8 (20 mins)

Example 2

In example 2, Tuesday, Wednesday and Thursday have two spaced practice sessions each in place of the single lesson. In terms of the total time spent on maths across a week, it's less that we might currently give it, but the impact of changing the way we structure things on learning could be significant. With example 1, the learning in maths would be 'reloaded' four times across the week at the beginning of each new session, but in example 2, there'd be seven occasions when the children were in the position of having to switch back into maths mode to reload whatever it was they were learning about.

There's no definitive answer in terms of how long the spaces should be, so it's something we can play around with. Given that the traditional lesson structures we've always used don't appear to support what's actually going on inside the children's heads, what's the worst that could happen?

Looking at spacing within a week is a good place to start, but to see long-term impact, we need to extend this thinking over greater chunks of time. If this is an example of what week 1 could look like, what about after that? To take advantage of this effect, the spaces need to get bigger, and in line with our desire to move from performance to learning, the support available will decrease. This perfect storm of desirable difficulty does exactly the opposite of what you'd expect, and instead of getting in the way of learning it actually enhances it. We might experience some short-term forgetting, but we need to see this as part of the process, rather than panicking and desperately topping it up. As strange as it sounds, over time, it turns out that the process of forgetting (and our management of it) is just as much a part of learning as remembering is.

The other deliberate action going on in example 2 is the scattering of maths over the whole of the timetable. I've had enough of the mornings being dominated by literacy and numeracy, and as far as I can see, there's no good reason why it needs to happen. If we're working on interconnected immersive projects, then relegating everything else to the afternoon slots sends the wrong message about how much we value them: 'We'll be doing our project work later, but we need to do English and maths first whilst you're still nice and awake!'

Even if English is woven into a project (and possibly maths too[4]), we can still be reluctant to break the morning/afternoon divide. But there's no rule about where things have to sit within a timetable, so having a much more flexible approach is within our grasp. We could even go as far as utilising the 'last thing on a Friday' slot, in which you might otherwise stick something like 'golden time' on the grounds that it's nearly the weekend. Because we don't need to be teaching them anything, the children can just get on with their self-directed practice and a calm end to the week is guaranteed – without the need to make them watch *Ice Age* for the twenty-first time.

---

4   I use the word 'possibly' because I'm a bit cautious with maths. English is always linked to a project because without it the children's writing wouldn't have a purpose or an audience. You can apply the same thinking to maths, but you have to work really hard to make it link, and even if you do, it's often tenuous and frequently unhelpful. The only time that maths can link to a project is at the point when the children have learnt the thing that we have been focusing on. At this point, a context can work well as a form of desirable difficulty: 'OK, I can see that you've learnt the process, but can you apply it to this …' A good example of this working well was in the Year 5 project on the Black Death that we looked at in Chapter 5 ('Do our choices really matter?'). After learning about rounding decimal numbers in maths, the children's depth of understanding was tested by presenting them with problems that revolved around ingredients for their own plague remedy. Each ingredient had a price which needed to be rounded to the nearest pound before finding a total.

To make the most of the idea of spacing, we also need to think about what to do with the gaps. This is where interleaving comes into play. The main thinking behind this is pretty simple: if we're leaving spaces between bits of learning or practice, then it's helpful to fill the gap with something so we're not just sitting around twiddling our thumbs. Most primary schools are already set up for this kind of operation thanks to the fact that we deliver such a wide range of different subjects and switching between them is unavoidable. This switching is also helpful in its own right because it doesn't leave us with any option other than to frequently reload the relevant pieces of learning. When we move from a little bit of maths to a little bit of history, then a little bit of RE, and then back to maths, the children are forced to remember whatever it was all over again.

Experimenting with this kind of thinking gives us the chance to approach the idea of timetabling with much more flexibility, and, more importantly, it helps to shift us from a purely organisational mindset to the kind of decision making that is entirely focused on learning.

Chapter 18

A SPANNER IN THE WORKS

The idea of desirable difficulties can also be applied on a much bigger scale. In the same way that adding awkwardness to the learning process can help to generate the conditions for creative thinking, there's no reason why we can't apply the same idea to disrupt the smooth running of a project. Helpfully, this process is made easier by the boldness of the project outcomes – the more adventurous they get, the more potential difficulties we'll come across.

In the Year 5 project, 'Do our choices really matter?' the outcome was a play that the children would perform at a theatre in Sheffield. It was based on the events in Eyam during the Black Death, and as well as starring in it, the children were also responsible for the script, production (including scenery, sound and lighting) and all the promotional activities. To help them piece together the story of the villagers, the teacher used a book called *The Children of Winter* by Berlie Doherty. The story is set in Eyam at the time of the plague and follows a group of children who, while sheltering from a storm in an old barn, find that they've slipped back in time to 1666. The book went down brilliantly with the children, and inspired their own stories and scripts that were honed and redrafted for their performance. While all of this was going on, the class teacher decided to tweet Berlie Doherty to let her know how much the class were enjoying the project and to say that they were using her book to help with their own performance. Within an hour or so, Berlie had tweeted back. The first part of the tweet was completely fine. She was delighted that the children were enjoying the book and that it was helping with the production of their play. It was the bit that followed that really caused the trouble. Along with making the lovely comments, Berlie also asked if she could come along and watch.

Your initial response might be that this is amazing news, and the teacher felt exactly the same way – right up until the reality of the situation began to sink in and she started to feel physically sick. This is not necessarily the kind of pressure that you want to be under as a teacher. It's hard enough putting together something good enough for parents, let alone a critical audience – or worse still, the very person who inspired the work in the first place. The anxiety about this was quickly resolved with the realisation that it wasn't her problem – it was the children's.

Their reaction was not that far removed from the teacher's. Initial excitement, quickly followed by the slowly dawning realisation of what this news actually meant. Almost instantly, thanks to the magic of social media, the children recognised that their work had to be better than they'd ever imagined. We discussed pressure earlier when we looked at developing outcomes, and this is a perfect example. The children weren't sobbing in a corner, they were determined. They wanted it to be perfect and this drove their desire to work at it until it was right.

There were definitely nerves on the night of the performance, but there was also a sense of accomplishment; the children knew they'd worked hard and they knew they were ready. Berlie and her husband sat front and centre in their VIP seats surrounded by the children's families and members of the community. The children were incredible – confident and professional. The sound and lighting team in the booth at the back nailed all their timings, the musical numbers were seamless and when the curtain came down at the end of the play, the applause was deafening. Berlie loved it, which was a good job given how much the children had invested in the whole thing, and the fact that she nipped backstage to speak to them personally only added to what was an experience they're never likely to forget.

This difficulty was really just a piece of luck. On another day, the teacher might not have had time to tweet and the project would have rolled to its conclusion without the children having to overcome this particular hurdle. Beyond this example, there are lots of other potential difficulties that stem directly from doing something 'real'. We've given Year 4 children the headache of how to build a wildlife pond on a piece of sloping land (and then consider how to make sure it was safe for the youngest children in the school), Year 5 children who needed to recoup the cost of hiring a gallery space because the quote was beyond what the school could afford, and Year 1 children who had to work out how to keep their animal sculptures made from natural materials fresh for long enough to make it to the exhibition (it was touch and go with the daisies).

These naturally occurring bits of awkwardness are traditionally the parts that we'd take care of as the teacher. There might be problems, but they'd be filtered out long before we were working with the children. In all of these examples, when a problem arose, it was a problem shared. It's not up to us to sort things out – we're in this together. This is helped along with a few magic words that aren't heard often enough in our classrooms: 'What do we think?' This one phrase communicates a shared stuckness. There's something up here and we need to sort it out: 'Has anyone got any ideas?'

In terms of creative thinking, the ability to overcome barriers, try out alternatives and adapt or develop ideas is exactly what the children will get to do if we leave the problems where they are and allow them to stumble into them. If the children are determined to be successful, they will find a way.

From time to time, there might be a project that's progressing a little too well for our liking. Maybe one of the naturally occurring difficulties sorted itself out or perhaps the solution was not as complicated as we'd hoped. In this case, we can just make it up. Manufacturing difficulties is a brilliant way of regulating the level of challenge within a project, and when pitched correctly, treads the fine line between difficult and insurmountable.

In the Year 6 project, 'How do we tell truth from tale?' the children worked together to curate an exhibition on aspects of Ancient China. Because of the focus on skills development, the children spent a long time interpreting and analysing primary and secondary sources, and as a result, generated a lot of information about their chosen area. Following this, they worked in groups to plan their exhibition. The children had some big ideas about what their work would look like, but this was before they were shown the exhibition space. What they were faced with was significantly less space than they'd imagined, and the type and shape of the display cabinets threw up further problems. They had to ask themselves, 'Do we go with a slightly larger table-top cabinet where everything would be together on one level, or a tall glass cabinet with three much smaller shelves?' This very deliberate act of teacher sabotage sent them back to the drawing board to rethink how best to use the restricted space they'd been given.

In a Year 3 geography-themed project that explored the question, 'What makes a community?' through the concepts of 'belonging', 'cohesion' and 'sustainability', the children began by designing their own community. This was left pretty open so they could include whatever entered their heads. The kind of stuff they came up with, unsurprisingly, was a fairly close replication of Disney World. They had roller coasters, water slides, parks and playgrounds, plus the odd house and roads that didn't go anywhere. After the initial designs, the teacher set about delivering a series of planned desirable difficulties that forced the children to develop their knowledge and understanding of how communities function, which then led them to think differently about their plan.

In our heads …	'I know you really like roller coasters, but we also need to think about essential services.'
	↓
Out loud …	'I wonder what would happen if there was an emergency?'

And then:

In our heads …	'The seven- to eight-year-old age bracket is pretty well catered for, but there are also other age groups to consider.'
	↓
Out loud …	'I wonder what kind of things we'd need to think about so that our community works for all of its members?'

And again:

In our heads ...	'OK, so we've thought about different age groups, but now I'd like us to explore other demographics.'
	↓
Out loud ...	'I wonder how we'd meet the needs of different cultures or faiths?'

And as a bit of follow-up awkwardness:

In our heads ...	'OK, so we're clear about different cultural and religious needs, but I'd now like to start unpicking the idea of community cohesion.'
	↓
Out loud ...	'If we only had space in our community for one place of worship, I wonder how it might work?'[1]

And before long, the children are wading through complex issues they'd never previously considered, and thanks to the conditions created by the teacher, they're pushed into exactly the kind of creative thinking that we set out to encourage from the start.

---

1   This is a perfect example of how children are better people than grown-ups. This is a difficulty but not an insurmountable problem – the idea of a shared place of worship seems to make perfect sense to eight-year-old minds. In fact, after thousands of years of worshipping separately, there is a project currently underway in Berlin called the House of One (https://house-of-one.org/en) that intends to solve exactly this problem. I wonder what local religious leaders would think of the project? Perhaps the children could ask.

Chapter 19

FREEDOM

The different aspects of a blended pedagogy take us a long way towards developing exactly the kind of learners we're after. At every stage of this process, for all of the reasons we've looked at, the teacher is right there in the thick of things. Sometimes it's obvious – through modelling or the layering of support to encourage independence – and sometimes it's much more subtle – the tiniest nudge that shifts the children into a different kind of thinking.

Arriving at this point leaves us with the question of whether there's any value in taking a step beyond this and stretching the concept of subtle intervention to include not really intervening at all. I suppose this would be the equivalent of letting the monkeys loose. If there was free rein, what would they get up to? And, more importantly, would it be worth the mess?

There are a few different approaches out there that allow this kind of freedom, and they all seem to follow a similar theme of dedicating time to allow children to be creative.

First of all, there's 'Creative Week', often in June – post SATs – which involves the whole school being imaginative. Things usually kick off with the head teacher telling the children in assembly that an alien has crash-landed in the school playground/the caretaker has been abducted/World War Three has started.[1] The teachers and children are then left to pick up the pieces and be creative for the rest of the week.

An alternative to the whole-school model is to take a weekly approach to freeing up the timetable for the children to do something different. Golden time got the briefest of mentions earlier, although, to be honest, it doesn't deserve a place here except for the fact that I've seen it being used as a way to give children the freedom to have a go at things they're interested in. It's more of a behaviour management weapon, which means a dedicated part of the timetable (usually up to an hour) is set aside as a reward. Children who've kept hold of their minutes get to choose to do an activity they like, and those who've lost their minutes by

---

1   This actually happened – just google 'head teacher World War Three'.

being naughty get to watch it all happening from the sidelines. Aside from the dubious intentions, it's generally dependent on whatever stuff the teacher decides to get out of their cupboard. Occasionally it might be great and you'll get to do exciting things with pipe cleaners, and sometimes it might just be the wet playtime colouring books, word searches or a DVD.

Genius hour is another idea that sets aside time for the children to follow their interests, but this time it's not tied to a behaviour strategy – the naughty kids are invited too.[2] As far as I can make out, it was started by Google who allowed its engineers to spend 20% of their time working on any project they fancied. The thinking behind it is that if people are allowed, or even encouraged, to work on a 'passion', they become more effective at the rest of their job. Apparently, this has worked so well that a significant chunk of Google's projects have been created thanks to this strategy, which suggests that perhaps there wasn't complete freedom in terms of how the time was spent. Whilst I would love to think there was someone sitting in the corner of Google HQ silently getting on with a spot of taxidermy, it's probably more likely that whatever they are up to bears some relevance to their role within the company.

In school, I've seen this idea adopted to allow the children to work on similarly autonomous projects. Usually, this involves deciding on a theme to explore, then working on it over a period of time (several weeks) before sharing it with the class or school. A variant of this is a Self-Organised Learning Environment (SOLE).[3] This idea was developed by Professor Sugata Mitra, who believes that children are smarter than we give them credit for. It all began in 1999 with his 'Hole in the Wall' experiment, which involved placing a computer in a kiosk in a Delhi slum and allowing children to play with it on their own. He found that they could learn to use a computer and the internet without being taught. In classrooms, this has translated into a very similar approach to the genius hour – rather than taking a spoon-feeding approach to learning, the children are encouraged to explore big ideas or un-google-able questions with minimal (or no) interaction from the teacher.

We'll ignore the first suggestion (Creative Week) for the reasons given on every single page of this book. Likewise, even if golden time happens to be a useful

---

2   See http://geniushour.com/what-is-genius-hour/.

3   See https://www.theschoolinthecloud.org.

behaviour management technique, it shouldn't be lumped into an attempt to generate creativity within the curriculum, so we'll gloss over that one too.

This leaves us with two suggestions that deserve a bit more consideration – genius hour and SOLE. They've both come in for some criticism from a particular group of educationalists who would rather we just tell children stuff (preferably in a firm/shouty voice). To dismiss these ideas out of hand is unnecessarily hasty, though, and whilst I agree with some of the criticisms, like most things in life, it's not as straightforward as it seems.

The issue that seems to get people all stirred up is the belief that the children don't learn anything and that whatever they end up producing is rubbish. This is a legitimate point, and can definitely be true of working in this way. In fact, I've seen it with my own eyes, and when it's bad, it's really, really bad. Most of the time, however, this is because the strategy has been implemented on a whim. It fills an awkward slot on the timetable and the children seem to like it.

The process involved in genius hour and SOLE is actually pretty simple: decide on a project or question that interests you and go for it. For it to be of any use, though, lots of elements need to be firmly embedded before we even think about setting the children off.

As far as intentions go, both approaches mirror the aims of the curriculum model we've been looking at in this book. They use an enquiry-based approach and aim to produce high quality work for a particular audience as an outcome. The starting point is usually a question. In the model we've been exploring, the question is developed to frame concepts which allow us to explore the curriculum content we're hoping to cover. This works because we're able to demonstrate how aspects of the curriculum link to both the concepts and the enquiry question; along with incorporating the children's thoughts, ideas and responses, we can make the connections explicit so that they see the bigger picture and begin to explore the project with the depth of knowledge and understanding we're after. This allows us to select for the kind of philosophical questions we've been considering.

Whilst you could attempt this using a SOLE-type model, there are a couple of things to be wary of. First, if we use a philosophical or un-google-able question, then we're likely to get a few different responses. If the children have some prior knowledge in their heads, then they can make a connection between this knowledge and the question. Alternatively, if there is limited or no knowledge in there (or if they don't make the connection because the question is too abstract), then they might use their imagination to give some immediate responses. A further reaction is to just google it. The fact that you might have called the question un-google-able is irrelevant because they won't believe you. For lots of them, there isn't anything you can't find out using the internet, and the fact that there will be some kind of response from the search engine – regardless of what question they type in – will be all the proof they need.[4]

These aren't necessarily problems – it's a good thing for children to be using their experiences and prior knowledge to make connections, and it's just as important for them to be using their imagination (and for us to be encouraging it). But what we need to be aware of is the possibility of it not moving beyond this, and if we're really interested in creativity, then there's got to be real substance too.

If we look at the question, 'How might we live in the future?' we can see how this might work in practice. First, we might get initial responses based on prior knowledge. This might come from books the children have read, films they've watched or relevant places they've visited. Tied in with this could also be responses that come from their imagination. It's actually quite difficult to have truly original thoughts without it being influenced by stuff we've seen or experienced before – when I think about living in the future it's all a bit *Star Wars/Blade Runner*. Having said that, because children haven't yet built up as many experiences as adults, they often find it easier than we do.

If the next stage is to google the question, then you get just under three billion results. To save some time, I've just gone for the top five:

1. Three ways technology will change the way we live in the future

2. London in 2060: how will we live in the future?

3. Back to the Future Day: six experts predict life in 2045

4. We are already living in the future

5. What will life be like in 2035?

Every one of these pages contains information that is linked to the question, and within a couple of clicks, we've got something that can be lifted and added to a poster or presentation ready to showcase to whoever might be watching. The

---

4 In reality, un-google-able means there's no definitive answer, but by the time you've tried to explain this to them they'll already be waving their search results in your face.

children would definitely be able to 'produce' something, and would probably enjoy themselves in the process, but I'm not convinced that it would be of much value.

For them to make a more informed response to the question, they need to have more to go on. This sounds fairly obvious, but it's not necessarily obvious to the children. This is where an abstract question can be quite tricky. Actually, there are other more tangible questions to be explored before beginning to think about what the future might be like, so without picking this apart or by relying on the children to realise this for themselves, we run the risk of only ever scratching the surface.

We could still begin in the same way, by collecting initial responses to our future question, but by breaking this down (or by helping the children to do so) we get several areas they can really get their teeth into:

- How do we live now?
- How do different communities and cultures live now?
- How have communities and societies changed in our lifetime?
- How have communities and societies changed in our parents' and grandparents' lifetime?

Developing answers to questions like these would provide a much deeper knowledge base for speculating about what life might be like in fifty or one hundred years' time, and even if the children still end up predicting that we'll be jetting around in flying cars, they will be doing so with the knowledge and understanding that this would be a continuation of the same kind of innovation that brought us steam trains and the internal combustion engine.

In terms of the children taking control of the process, once they are clear about useful starting points, it would make sense for them to adopt the same approaches they've used successfully in previous projects. For example, if they've decided to begin by researching the question, 'How do we live now?' they could use the process of critique to ensure that the outcome of this research reflects the kind of quality we're expecting.

If they have decided to present their findings in a report, then they would need to begin by seeking out a range of exemplars as a starting point. Next, they would go through the process of generating the feedback needed to create a rubric. With the rubric in place, they could then begin to develop their work – creating, critiquing and redrafting as they go along. When we add into the mix a culture of producing brilliant work (because that's what they're up to on a daily basis) and the knowledge that they have access to a range of expertise (including us!), then there's an extremely high chance that the children will work with real purpose, determination and creativity.

If we want to allow the children to have the freedom to decide for themselves what they want to learn about, rather than being given a question (the genius hour model), then guiding them towards less abstract questions or starting points would seem to be a useful strategy. Regardless of how far we might take this, it's still not a completely hands-off approach – there is freedom but within a well-defined structure. We've taught the children how to self-regulate by planning, monitoring and evaluating their learning, and now we're seeing if they can apply it to different contexts. If we were desperate for a name, we could call it metacognitive mastery.

If the children understand what's involved in producing excellent work, then genius hour and SOLE can be useful additions to the range of opportunities we give our children. It's not about just leaving them to it and hoping for the best, because if we're truly interested in our children developing self-regulating strategies and skills, then we've got to let go of the reins. When we looked at learning, we deliberately set out to wean the children off the layers of support. The end goal was to completely remove the scaffolding so they could do whatever it was independently. If we're applying this thinking to *what* the children are learning, then why not also apply it to the *how*? The ideal situation for something like critique is for it to be so well embedded (or learnt) that the children become truly autonomous, and gradually building freedom through approaches like this can be a very useful way to do it.

Increased autonomy is the ultimate aim of a curriculum that has creativity and independence at its heart. It's easy to get distracted by the shiny, glittery, creative bits, but if we've started with the hard work (and the hard thinking), then this final layer of freedom becomes a possibility. If we really believe that working in this way has an impact on our young people, then we should be brave enough to put it to the test. When we set our little monkeys free, do they go wild and poo all over the carpet, or do they set about creating something amazing?

CONCLUSION

When we set out our stall at the beginning of this book, we had some pretty bold aims:

Our curriculum is skills based and knowledge rich; we cover less because we believe that our children should have the opportunity to study areas of the curriculum in greater depth. We want our children to produce exceptional outcomes whilst developing their independence, curiosity and creativity. We want to produce collaborators, innovators, leaders and, more than anything else, young people who understand what it means to be human.

These are the words that sit at the top of my school's curriculum policy and they were written as a statement of intent. But a curriculum isn't just a document, or at least it shouldn't be. Choosing to work differently is a commitment to action. There are plenty of people out there who dismiss the aim of developing creative thinking, independence and curiosity as a hopeless waste of time, but these people underestimate the determination that dedicated individuals like us have to show that it can and does work. We have to think hard about it, and we have to work hard at it, but there is another way.

BIBLIOGRAPHY

Berger, R. (2003) *An Ethic of Excellence: Building a Culture of Craftsmanship with Students* (Portsmouth, NH: Heinemann).

Biesta, J. J. G. (2013) *The Beautiful Risk of Education* (Boulder, CO: Paradigm Publishers).

Biggs, J. and Collis, K. (1982) *Evaluating the Quality of Learning: The SOLO Taxonomy* (New York: Academic Press).

Bjork, E. L. and Bjork, R. A. (2011) Making Things Hard on Yourself, but in a Good Way: Creating Desirable Difficulties to Enhance Learning. In M. A. Gernsbacher, R. W. Pew, L. M. Hough and J. R. Pomerantz (eds), *Psychology and the Real World: Essays Illustrating Fundamental Contributions to Society* (New York: Worth Publishers), pp. 56–64.

Bjork, R. A. (2013) Desirable Difficulties Perspective on Learning. In H. Pashler (ed.), *Encyclopedia of the Mind* (Thousand Oaks, CA: Sage Reference), pp. 243–245.

Brunton, P. and Thornton, L. (2010) *Bringing the Reggio Approach to Your Early Years Practice* (Abingdon: Routledge).

Carey, B. (2014) *How We Learn: The Surprising Truth About When, Where, and Why It Happens* (London: Macmillan).

Centre for Education Statistics and Evaluation (2017) *Cognitive Load Theory: Research That Teachers Really Need to Understand* (Sydney: New South Wales Department of Education).

Department for Education (2013) *National Curriculum in England: Key Stages 1 and 2 Framework Document* (London: DfE).

Doherty, B. (2007 [1985]) *Children of Winter* (London: Catnip Publishing).

Duckworth, A. L. (2013) Grit: The Power of Passion and Perseverance [video], *TED.com*. Available at: https://www.ted.com/talks/angela_lee_duckworth_grit_the_power_of_passion_and_perseverance/.

Dweck, C. S. (2017) *Mindset: Changing the Way You Think to Fulfil Your Potential* (London: Robinson).

Education Endowment Foundation (2018) *Metacognition and Self-Regulated Learning: Guidance Report* (London: EEF). Available at: https://educationendowmentfoundation.org.uk/evidence-summaries/teaching-learning-toolkit/meta-cognition-and-self-regulation.

Ellicott, C. and Wright, S. (2015) The 'Swarm' on Our Streets, *Daily Mail* (31 July).

Gerver, R. (2010) *Creating Tomorrow's Schools Today* (London: Continuum).

Gilbert, I. (2018) *The Working Class: Poverty, Education and Alternative Voices* (Carmarthen: Independent Thinking Press).

Gilbert, I. (2015) *There Is Another Way: The Second Big Book of Independent Thinking* (Carmarthen: Independent Thinking Press).

Hattie, J. and Yates, G. (2014) *Visible Learning and the Science of How We Learn* (Abingdon: Routledge).

Heathcote, D. (1984) *Collected Writings on Education and Drama* (London: Hutchinson & Co.).

Henriques, G. (2013) What Is Knowledge? A Brief Primer, *Psychology Today* (4 December). Available at: https://www.psychologytoday.com/intl/blog/theory-knowledge/201312/what-is-knowledge-brief-primer.

Hurston, Z. N. (1942) *Dust Tracks on a Road: An Autobiography* (London: Hutchinson & Co.).

Lear, J. (2015) *Guerrilla Teaching: Revolutionary Tactics for Teachers on the Ground, in Real Classrooms, Working with Real Children, Trying to Make a Real Difference* (Carmarthen: Independent Thinking Press).

McKenna, D. (2016) Eyam Plague: The Village of the Damned, *BBC News* (5 November). Available at: https://www.bbc.co.uk/news/uk-england-35064071.

Mitra, S. and Dangwal, R. (2010) Limits to Self-Organising Systems of Learning: The Kalikuppam Experiment, *British Journal of Educational Technology* 41(5): 672–688.

Morpurgo, M. (2017 [1999]) *Kensuke's Kingdom* (London: Egmont).

Myatt, M. (2016) *High Challenge, Low Threat: How the Best Leaders Find the Balance* (Woodbridge: John Catt Educational).

PSHE Association (2017) *Programme of Study for PSHE Education (Key Stages 1–5)* (London: PSHE Association). Available at: https://www.pshe-association.org.uk/system/files/PSHE%20Education%20Programme%20of%20Study%20%28Key%20stage%201-5%29%20Jan%202017_2.pdf.

Qualifications and Curriculum Authority (2011) A Framework of Personal Learning and Thinking Skills. Available at: http://webarchive.nationalarchives.gov.uk/20110215111658/http://curriculum.qcda.gov.uk/key-stages-3-and-4/skills/personal-learning-and-thinking-skills/index.aspx.

Quigley, A. (2018) *Closing the Vocabulary Gap* (Abingdon: Routledge).

Sharratt, N. (2007) *Caveman Dave* (London: Walker Books).

Sheffield SACRE (2014) *Enquiring Minds & Open Hearts: Religious Education for All. The Agreed Syllabus for RE in Sheffield 2014–2019.* Available at: http://www.learnsheffield.co.uk/Downloads/Partnerships/SACRE%20Agreed%20Syllabus%202014%20-%202019.pdf.

Sweller, J., Ayres, P. and Kalyuga, S. (2011) *Cognitive Load Theory* (New York: Springer).

Wagner, B. J. (1999) *Dorothy Heathcote: Drama as a Learning Medium* (Portland, ME: Calendar Islands Publishers).

INDEX

Guerrilla Teaching

Revolutionary tactics for teachers on the ground, in real classrooms, working with real children, trying to make a real difference

Jonathan Lear

ISBN: 978-178135232-8

Guerrilla Teaching is a revolution. Not a flag-waving, drum-beating revolution, but an underground revolution, a classroom revolution. It's not about changing policy or influencing government; it's about doing what you know to be right, regardless of what you're told. It's sound advice for people on the ground: people in real classrooms, working with real children, trying to make a real difference. *Guerrilla Teaching* by Jonathan Lear is packed with ideas to refresh teaching practice – combining direct teaching with creative child-led learning – and forge cross-curricular links to create engaging, motivating and fun learning experiences. Ultimately, *Guerrilla Teaching* is about making a difference. It's a book Jonathan Lear never meant to write, but it was just too important not to.

Filled with thoughts, ideas and strategies that will help to develop creativity and creative thinking in the primary classroom, *Guerrilla Teaching* is for trainee teachers, new teachers, teaching assistants, experienced teachers and head teachers – there's something for everyone!